Outfoxing
the Small  Business
Owner

*Crafty Techniques for
Creating a Profitable Relationship*

Gene Marks
• • • • • • • • • • •

Adams Media
Avon, Massachusetts

Published by Adams Media, an F+W Publications Company
57 Littlefield Street
Avon, MA 02322 U.S.A.
www.adamsmedia.com

ISBN: 1-59337-157-8

Printed in Canada

J I H G F E D C B A

Library of Congress Cataloging-in-Publication Data
Marks, Gene.
Outfoxing the small business owner / Gene Marks.
p.   cm.
ISBN 1-59337-157-8
1. Industrial marketing. 2. Small business. 3. Self-employed.
4. Family-owned business enterprises. 5. Entrepreneurship. I. Title.
HF5415.1263.M36 2004
658.8'04--dc22

2004013277

Interior illustration by Dave Winter

Dedication

To my fellow small business owners everywhere.

Acknowledgments

Thanks to my father Ronald Marks and to Vicki Bralow, David Graham, and Alan Weiss for their excellent advice, comments, and help in writing this book. Thanks also to my agent, Michael Snell for believing in this idea and to my editor Jill Alexander for working her magic. It was David Pressel's urging over dinner a few years back that motivated me to start down this path.

But it was Angela, my wife and best friend, and her unwavering confidence in me that was the real force behind this book. Don't worry, I'm not going to get all mushy!

Table of Contents

Introduction: Crazy Like a Fox

Say Hello to the Fox

Have you had experience in selling products or services to both small businesses and large corporations? If so, you probably have already seen how different the two types of relationships can be. With small businesses, you are likely to be dealing with a driven entrepreneur who is engaged in every aspect of his company and who works endless hours just to survive; with large companies, you might be making an appointment with one of the seventeen vice-presidents hanging on to the corporate ladder. It's the noble (though sometimes exasperating) small business owner who is the hero of our tale, so let's allow him to introduce himself in his own words.

I'm a fox, otherwise known to the layperson as a small business owner or entrepreneur. And I bet you're working morning, noon, and night to make me happy. Pretty frustrating, isn't it? Well, I'm pretty smart. I've survived more than a decade out on my own, without a job. I can be pretty crazy sometimes. And occasionally I can be a rascal as well.

I really don't have the time to talk to you, or pay attention to your promotions. I'm too busy being everything to everybody in my own company. I have no help, just people making demands of me. I'm sometimes flush, but most of the time I'm short of cash. I want the best that money can buy as long as it's dirt-cheap. I'm going to take up your time with lots of questions then forget half of what you told me so I can ask you again at a later date. I'm going to delay and defer any decision until it's absolutely necessary. Sometimes when you call me I may abruptly end the conversation. And if you visit me in my out-of-the-way, fairly dilapidated office space, don't be surprised to see me yelling amidst the chaos of my business.

Don't call me unless I call you. But when I do call, make sure you're instantly available and ready to solve my problem. Because when I call it's because I've got a problem that needs solving right now. In fact, it should have been solved a few months ago like you told me. But now it's *really* a problem. So send your best people out here right away—and if you don't respond immediately I'll yell and scream until you do. I'm going to behave like I'm the size of IBM and General Motors rolled into one. I'm used to that kind of response from my own employees, and I'll expect the same from you. And don't try to take advantage of me, because I'll be watching. Just fix my problem with your product or service as quickly as possible and keep the bill low.

Oh, and by the way, I'm not going to pay your bill on time either. Don't worry—it'll get paid eventually. I'm a man of my word. It's just that I'm probably going to have other, more pressing bills to pay when yours comes due. So you'll just have to wait. You may have to entice the money out of me. You may have to call me a few times to remind me. You may even get a little annoyed at me when I stretch things out a few months. Hey pal, I'm a small business owner and I've got my own bank account to worry about. I'm trying to manage a million things at once, and your invoice is not a high priority with me today. I realize you made me a priority when I needed you the most. Thanks. I'll definitely get you a few dollars sometime this week. And then we can work out the rest, okay?

You still love me, don't you? You must, because you keep coming back for more. You're convinced that there must be some way to make a profit off of me. You just haven't quite figured out how to do it yet.

Yes, I'm a fox. And there are about seventeen million of us small business foxes out here. Just think of the opportunity. If you were to get a single dollar from only 6 percent of us you would earn a million bucks! If you could convince only 1 percent of us to give you just two measly dollars every year then you'd be earning way more than a quarter of a million dollars annually. How hard can that be?

Very hard, actually, because I'm not going to give you that dollar. It's my dollar and I want to keep it in my bank account. I'm not some worker at a corporation. I don't clock out at 5:00 P.M. and forget about my job. I don't just get handed a paycheck as long as I receive a good evaluation from my boss. I don't have dozens of other people around me making sure I'm not goofing up. There's no corporate budget that I can exceed. I don't make decisions just because I think it'll please the president. I *am* the president. Every dollar my company spends is one less dollar in my pocket. You're going to have to fight me tooth and nail for that dollar.

And, if by chance, I spend my dollar on you I'm never going to let you forget it. I'm going to make you earn that dollar. Every penny of it. I'm going to call for service frequently—I don't have time to read the instructions or a manual. And I don't have the patience to wait long for an answer either. I'm going to try and get more product or service than I actually deserve for my dollar, too. If you're in customer service you better be ready to handle the likes of me.

If you're not careful, you may spend $2 just to get my $1. Foxes like me can be pretty tough to handle. If your sales or service organization is not structured to address my needs then I'm going to go somewhere else. I'm pretty smart. And crazy, too. Crazy like a fox.

But we foxes are also good customers! We're very loyal. We appreciate other foxes. We have respect for people who do a good job for a fair price. We work very hard. We can make decisions in a snap and react quickly to problems. We can bend the rules to get things done. We care so much about what we do that we think about it day and night. Our employees are our friends and we move mountains to look out for them. Our best suppliers are our partners and we have close relationships with them. We employ 98 percent of the people in this country and create millions of new jobs every year. We put our reputation on the line every day and depend on it for our survival.

And survive we do. The fox is an adaptable creature. Foxes spring up in all kinds of places. Even the most poverty-stricken countries have countless clever and wily foxes earning a living for their families. We are the oldest profession, and we produce the newest technologies. We fall down and we get back up again. Most of us stop what we're doing only when we die. We never give up. We drove America's industrial revolution, and we're the soul of today's worldwide economy.

We are manufacturers, lawyers, telecommunications experts, distributors, wholesalers, contractors, designers, consultants, technologists, educators, repairmen, restaurateurs, shopkeepers, healthcare providers, transporters, financiers, advisors, publishers, marketers, builders, and destructors. There are millions of us, and we challenge you to make us happy.

Are you prepared to do business with a foxy small business owner? Do you have thick skin? Are you flexible? Can you be patient? Do you have a good sense of humor? Are you resourceful? Can you adapt quickly? Will you be my partner?

Small business owners are not like your corporate customers. We have different demands. We keep a different schedule. We care a lot more about some things and a lot less about other things. We don't share the same priorities. We don't have the same needs. We are foxes. They are not.

So what's the matter? You can't get my attention to show me your product or service? You're spending too much money to get me to say yes? You feel like you can never please me? I don't pay you on time? You can't figure out a way to make more profit off of my kind? Don't despair. I can be sold to. I can be happily serviced. I can be a very profitable customer for you. And fun to work with, too. Come into my den and let me teach you how!

Show Me the Money

*Why Selling to the Resourceful Fox
Is a Unique Experience*

Before I started my own business, I spent almost nine years at an international accounting and consulting firm that primarily dealt with multinational companies. These clients were a far cry from the small business foxes I would be selling to in my new venture. And boy, was I unprepared to deal with one of my first small business prospects.

Ray was the owner of a company called Transitol Manufacturing, and he was a real wily fox. I was drawn into Ray's lair when one of our telemarketers interested him in an accounting software application we sold. Being new to the world of wily foxes, I spoke briefly to Ray on the phone and quickly set up a visit, figuring that I would show him the software and pick up a check. At the time, the software cost about $5,000, a mere pittance compared to the multimillion dollar projects I had worked on in my previous corporate life. Selling to a small business guy like Ray would be a piece of cake!

My first hint that things would not go as smoothly as planned was the condition of Ray's building when I drove up—or should I say, down—to it. It took me a while to find it. There was no sign or indication that a business existed anywhere on the residential street that bore his address. In fact, Ray's little shop occupied a worn-down structure located at the bottom of a very windy driveway. It was hidden from view and probably not legally zoned. Given its out-of-the-way location, the empty barrels and rusted parts strewn about, as well as the unused piles of rubbish among the weeds surrounding the building I imagined that Ray wasn't anxious for a visit from environmental or licensing agents any time soon.

I felt especially out of place in the suit I was wearing when Ray greeted me in cutoff shorts and a tie-dyed shirt. There was no receptionist, but I did notice a couple of women chatting over a pile of paperwork in a room off the main area. Ray told me that one of the women was his wife, who worked part-time doing the books while their kids were in school. Considering some of the elaborately equipped, multimedia conference rooms and office facilities of the larger companies where I used to work, I thought that Ray must be kind of embarrassed to take visitors into a dimly lighted, musty-smelling extra office. He didn't show it, though, as he chatted while moving stacks of paper and half-filled boxes out of the way so I could sit on one of the 1950s-style lawn chairs that made up his conference room.

My concern quickly turned to annoyance when our conversation was interrupted by phone calls and intrusions by other employees claiming one problem or another. I was further frustrated with Ray's overall lack of professionalism. He used obscenities, for goodness sake! And his manner was pretty gruff too, asking me to "get to the point" and wasting little time before asking about the price of my software. I was completely unable to use the great selling techniques I had spent half my career learning, developing, and refining. Although I expected to get a check from him that day, he made what I thought to be a relatively small purchase seem like a major expenditure. He moaned about the expense. He complained about his high overhead and the people who never showed up for work. He cried about the overall state of the economy. It was quite a performance. I left without my check, but with a promise to "think about it." This sale was not exactly the piece of cake I thought it would be.

Ray did think about it. For three years. He said he read the materials I sent to him but he kept asking me the same questions again and again. He had two free expert consultants: me, and his brother in law who owned a home computer. He avoided my calls for months on end. He requested references but never called them. He repeatedly kept asking if we offered any discounts. He wasn't sure if buying an accounting software program was worth it. So he got me to send him analysis, white papers, and other articles—also for free. He kept asking to get together, and when he wasn't being interrupted we went over the same questions again and again. He referred me to his wife, and she referred me back to him. I probably spent fifty hours trying to get Ray to buy a $5,000 software product. And he never did buy it. As far as I know, Ray has the same old system and is doing things the same way he has always done them or he used what he learned from my free consulting to buy elsewhere.

What a fool I was! My entire sales approach wasn't geared to a wily small business owner like Ray. It was something out of a textbook, more suitable for larger companies. I learned that if I didn't change what I was doing, and quick, I'd be out of business myself.

What the Big Guys Have Discovered

The first lesson I learned was this: The corporate clients I used to sell to were just not like the resourceful and sometimes crafty small business customer. Those foxes really knew how to exploit a prospective resource who wanted their business. Continuing to treat small business owners the same as corporate clients would be a big mistake! I wish I had known this sooner. I could have avoided a lot of time wasted pursuing the Rays of the business world. I should have looked at some of the more well-known companies and how they do business. They know that the small business marketplace is its own industry.

Foxy FACT

In 2002, there were approximately 22.9 million small businesses in the United States, according to Small Business Administration estimates.

Giants That Do It Well

Why does American Express have services specifically for small businesses and merchants and separate services for corporations? Why does Dell Computer break down its product lines between "home and home office," "small businesses," and "medium and large businesses"? Why are most products and services from successful technology companies like Oracle, Siebel, and Sybase virtually unknown to small businesses? Why, on the other hand, are offerings from Intuit, Microsoft, and Hewlett-Packard recognizable to the general consumer? Why do you rarely see a big consulting firm like Price Waterhouse or IBM working with your mechanic, heating contractor, or landscaping service?

These companies, and many others like them, have recognized that selling to the small business marketplace requires a very different model. A special skill set is required.

Companies that have entered into the small business market and hoped to apply a formula that worked well in the corporate world have learned the hard way that the rules are not the same. Oracle Corporation has continuously fallen short in its attempt to market small business accounting software. Exxon Corporation never quite got it right with its Qyx word processing venture in the late 1970s. Numerous telecommunications companies have bitten the dust in recent years trying to be the answer for both small and corporate customers alike.

Foxy **TIP**

Want to know why most small businesses stay small? Read The E-Myth Revisited *by Michael Gerber and you'll find out with whom you're dealing.*

Do Prudential Insurance, Citigroup, or Merck approach their larger accounts like their smaller customers? Definitely not. They have specially trained salespeople designated to handle each respective market. They have built separate infrastructures to handle large and small customers. Pricing, service arrangements, and procedures are completely different. Companies like these understand that doing business with small businesses is unique. They have shaped their organizations to handle the small business marketplace effectively. If you want to avoid mistakes, follow the lead of companies who got it right.

Recognizing the Small Business

The most important thing companies that operate successfully in the small business marketplace know is that you need to define your customer. You need to separate the wily foxes from the large bears. These companies have come up with an internal definition of a "small business customer" and dedicated a part of their organization to sell and service that type of customer. The most important step is to define what a small business is. Here are a few ways to quickly classify and identify them.

Revenues

Many people say that the most common way to define a small business is by revenue. Unfortunately, the typical mom-and-pop outfit is unlikely to disclose their revenue to you right away. You're going to have to make a judgment call. Try to get a range of annual sales. Generally, an operation that grosses less than $10 million in annual revenue would fall into the small business category. But remember that although revenue size is important it may not be the definitive answer. There are other attributes that should also be considered.

Foxy TIP

Never ask for specific revenue numbers from a small business owner. Instead, use a range (i.e., less than $1 million annually) to gauge their size.

Employees

Companies that sell to the small business market often define their customers by the number of employees. Many characterize a small business as employing fewer than 250 people. However, there is a range here. Companies with fewer than 2,500 employees can fall into the "small and medium business" classification. The companies that I talk about in this book all have fewer than fifty people. Most have fewer than ten. They're mom-and-pop businesses. Ray, for example, employs about twenty people at Transitol and is included in my definition of a small business. A good rule of thumb is if a small business becomes large enough to require a full-time human resources person they are most likely no longer a small business.

Foxy **FACT**

Eighty-nine percent of all U.S. companies have fewer than 20 employees.

Family

Foxes tend to run in packs. Family firms comprise 80 to 90 percent of all business enterprises in North America. Unfortunately, in many family-run businesses family members are too busy squabbling with each other to really manage effectively. Often, people are brought into a business when their most important qualification is that they're a family member—not because they possess superior business skills. This type of nepotism can limit a family-owned business and keep it in the small potatoes league. Most of the time this is okay with the family running the business. They just want to make a good living for all.

Larger companies are usually not family run. Sure there are exceptions, such as Comcast Corporation, Ford Motor, and the Mars Candy Company. But the lion's share of big companies have

MBA-trained executives and management recruited from different parts of the world based on their experience and specialties, not because they're married to the controller.

Ownership

A small business is generally owned by one person, or a very small group of people. In fact, a 1992 study determined that 73 percent of all small businesses were operated by their original founders. Some small businesses may be backed by venture capital firms. These are not your typical mom-and-pop shops. They might start out small but the intention is to become a big company in a short period of time. As I'll discuss later in this book, a start-up that has one or more venture capital firms funding it should be treated differently than the typical small business. For the most part, a small business is like Transitol—solely owned and operated. Ray had purchased the company from his uncle fifteen years before and never looked back. Many times a small business is run by one person with a few silent, minority investors, such as relatives who lent the owner a few bucks for seed capital twenty years before.

Larger companies, on the other hand, tend to have many owners. Many of them are publicly held. Still more are owned by investment banks, mutual funds, limited partnerships, and bondholders.

Information

Many small business owners share a common trait. They tend to fly beneath the radar. For example, a guy like Ray at Transitol tries to avoid the limelight. He stays clear of the government. He doesn't like to pay taxes, and he detests paperwork. He loathes workmen's compensation, sales and use taxes, safety regulations, and environmental protection standards. He likes to lay low, do his business quietly, and avoid any unnecessary attention. As a result, information about him is somewhat scarce. So is he being a crafty fox or a crazy one?

Foxy **TIP**

Finding data about your small business customer is tough. To get a good jump on your research, start at the search engine at www.business.com.

Information about larger companies is more readily available. The bigger the organization, the more attention they receive. Information about larger companies can be easily found on the Internet, through brokerage houses, credit agencies, and other research organizations.

Perks

Small business owners are smart and resourceful, and they don't waste their money on the perks and trappings normally seen at a big company. For example, they're ingenious at finding ways to avoid the overhead of a human relations or personnel department, company cars for their employees, stock ownership plans, excessive training, formal vacation and sick day policies, company libraries, and a mail room.

At a small business you probably won't see an employee bulletin board, an internal help desk, computers newer than three years old, floral arrangements or interior decorating, a company magazine or newsletter, a cafeteria, or decent lighting. Small business customers would rarely stomach annual picnics, United Way fund drives, name tags, login books, sponsorships, corner offices, administrative assistants, safety programs, contingency plans, highly paid consultants, people with titles, clean bathrooms, or landscaping work on their property. Mom-and-pop businesses like to keep their expenses down. All of the above cost too much money. To sell and service the crazy fox you need to show him or her that more money will be returned than spent; otherwise, just forget about it!

Facility

Transitol's dusty meeting room says it all. There are no fresh flowers, oak furniture, floor-to-ceiling windows, or state-of-the-art phone and computer equipment. His coffee machine is old and produces one flavor only. There is no beaming receptionist who is always on duty. There are no groups of men and women in smart business suits striding importantly through the well-lighted corridors.

Foxy TIP

Want to always reach those foxes? Get a cell phone number from them early in your relationship and keep it on file. More and more small business owners can't live without their cell phone.

A big company will usually invest in its facility. Appearance is very important. It contributes to the company's image and credibility in its marketplace. It's expected that a larger company will have decent facilities—otherwise, people begin to wonder about its financial position. Ray survives by keeping his overhead low. That's what foxes do.

First Impressions

Small business owners often answer their own phone. If you call Transitol before 8:00 A.M., or after 6:00 P.M., you'll probably get Ray on the line. Chances are extremely slim that Warren Buffett will pick up the main line at Berkshire Hathaway no matter what time of day you call. Ray has a love-hate relationship with his phone. Every time the phone rings it's either a problem or an opportunity. An employee is calling in sick, or a prospect is calling for a quote. A delivery truck is down with engine problems, or that big job just came through. Ray has people who answer the phone for him, but sometimes they're busy, or just not around. And he's not going to let the phone just ring.

You Can't Believe This Is a Business!

The real objective of a wily fox like Ray is to profitably operate his little business somewhere off the radar screen of the government and others that he believes want to take advantage of him. It's unlikely that some 500-person organization in a large plant near the highway is unknown to you. But what about that little business of twenty people operating out of that building you thought was condemned? Who would have thought? There are lots of opportunities to make a few bucks out there, and you're going to bump into creative little foxes everywhere making a go of it. Small companies like to occupy niches. There are niches so small that a larger corporation could never work in them successfully or turn a profit. But with low overhead and some fancy footwork, a resourceful little rascal like Ray knows how to eke out a few bucks and keep a couple of dozen people on the payroll.

A large corporate entity takes some raw materials and creates a highly specialized paper product that's used throughout the world. But the results of this creation don't end there. Making this product creates remnants. And the little company buys these remnants from the larger company, re-rolls it and then resells this scrap to an after-market of other unknown companies. It's simply amazing, the many ways that small companies can make money.

Foxy **TIP**

A derelict building may house a little goldmine. Don't be deceived by the looks of a small company's offices.

Small Business Customers Are Different from Large Customers

Now that we've identified what a small business is, it's important to know just why your small business prospects and customers are different from their larger, corporate counterparts. Knowing these differences will significantly help in selling and servicing them.

The Resource Problem

The average small business has a net income of 6.3 percent of revenues. For a company grossing $1 million a year, that's not a lot left over!

A crazy fox has fewer resources than a larger company. The small business owner can't just create a committee to evaluate a potential new piece of equipment. They aren't going to form a group to run a project. They don't have in-house attorneys to pore over contracts or a financial staff to do analysis. There are very few individuals around to help manage the company. The fox must think on his feet and take his chances. He does not have enough space to keep good files and documentation. He runs a greater risk of failure because he can rarely do the type of due diligence on a purchase that a larger company can accomplish. He is the president, director of marketing, vice president of sales, purchasing manager, and general manager. He must be familiar enough with all of these specialties to at least keep his business on track. Can you or your product be that resource that he doesn't have?

"Show Me the Money"

Not only do small business owners have fewer resources, they also have less money to throw around. *Every* purchase is a significant purchase. *Every* mistake could be a big one. They can't afford significant cost overruns. They rarely compare actual expenditures versus a budget. They look at what's been spent versus what's left in the bank. A typical wheeler-dealer like Ray at Transitol is much more obsessed over actual cash outlays than his corporate counterpart, because every dime leaving the account is *his* money. A corporate manager may be evaluated for line item fiscal responsibility, but he is also evaluated for other things, too—management skills, teamwork, loyalty, attendance, ability to work with others, organizational skills, and sometimes even his golf game.

Ray, on the other hand, is evaluated by no one but his customers. And his customers don't check off performance review forms and make recommendations for promotions. If satisfied, they pay him and then come back for more. If unsatisfied, they don't. It's always "show me the money" in the small business owner's eyes, nothing else. Will your product or service put money into his account?

Take This Job and Shove It!

One thing's for sure: Ray doesn't wake up in the morning thinking of ways to sneak into work late so his boss doesn't notice. He knows that if he's not there then things won't get done. And if they don't get done it's not like he continues to get his paycheck. He understands that putting money in the bank depends almost entirely on his effort, and this keeps him going even when there's no energy left. Running a small business is a livelihood. Bad decisions affect him directly, not someone else in some other department in the Kansas City branch. Ray knows that every purchase and each sale affect his bottom line. A lot of employees care only about quitting time, but a small business owner wants to get the most productivity and profit out of every day. Your objective is to help the small business owner like Ray do his work better and more quickly.

Foxy TIP

Maintain a very flexible schedule and be prepared to make changes for the chaotic small business customer. Always call ahead to confirm visits. Small business owners, you'll find, are always on the run.

Management by Doing

An astute fox like Ray is someone who gets things done. He doesn't like red tape. He doesn't like to waste time. He's busy putting out so many fires that he can't be put on hold, fill out unnecessary forms, or go through layers of people to get an answer. He knows what everyone else in his company is doing, because what they're doing ultimately affects his fate. Ray's not a paper pusher;

he tries to be a paper stopper. He dislikes the government and all of its regulations. He complains about all the time he spends doing administrative work instead of actual productive work. He's frustrated by the layers of bureaucracy he must endure and how costly this is to his company. Will you be able to help him cut to the chase and get things done?

Crazy Like a Fox

To reach a certain level at a large company, you'll pretty much need college and even graduate degrees. You'll probably hold some sort of industry or professional certification and regularly attend conferences and other training sessions. No such requirements are needed to run a small business. In fact, you'll meet many clever and crazy foxes that have never been to college and could not care less about any professional certifications. Ray's lack of formal education is well compensated for by his perceptiveness and street smarts for making a few bucks. Remember not to underestimate a guy like Ray . . . because that's exactly what he wants. He's crazy like a fox!

Get to the Point

There's a scene in the movie *Pulp Fiction*, where Mr. Wolf, a respected underworld "cleanup man," is hired to help two thugs take care of a very messy murder scene inside a car. Mr. Wolf is a very direct man with a job to do. He immediately begins to bark out orders. When one of the thugs, Vincent, doesn't like the gruff tone used, Mr. Wolf replies sweetly to him "Pretty please, with sugar on top, clean the &%@^* car!" This is what a small business owner does. Just like Mr. Wolf (and our friend Ray), they are more direct. Ray likes to cut to the chase. And sometimes he comes off as brusque, rude, and unprofessional. Ray doesn't have formal management training. And people skills may not be his strong suit. He just wants to get things done and move on to the next fire. Don't be put off by a Mr. or Ms. Wolf. Just help them finish the job.

Lack of Control

Typical of most small companies, Transitol has far less financial and organizational control than a larger company. There are few separations of duties. Ray's wife writes the checks, collects the cash, and also does the bank reconciliations (this is a major faux pas in the world of internal controls). A vendor's invoice can be approved or delayed on his whim without further questioning. Paperwork follows a general path but is easily mislaid or lost. There are not enough people to safeguard inventory. Receivables may stay open longer than desired because there is no collection system is in place. The flow of transactions may be severely interrupted when Ray decides to take a vacation. Personal expenditures often find themselves in the company's books. Important documents get misfiled without copies. Decisions are made and, if undocumented, forgotten. The important stuff gets done—eventually. But often Ray needs to be reminded by outsiders when a bill has to be paid or a commitment is coming due. Can you help bring some order into his place?

Small Potatoes

As unpredictable as he may be, Ray still has much less influence over his vendors than does a larger company. He can't dangle the promise of riches to come when it's so obvious that his long-term purchases will have a limit. He can't promise other work from additional subsidiaries and divisions. In the eyes of his vendors, he's small potatoes, and he knows it. The large company can leverage off its prestige. Its name on a vendor's customer list is a selling point, and it knows that the vendor is willing to negotiate for the privilege of doing business with it. Bigger corporations can take the time to do something that most small businesses cannot: have primary and secondary vendors. They can play their vendors off each other, getting multiple bids and negotiating separate deals. Our hero barely has enough time to find *one* good vendor, let alone build a contact list of multiple resources. And after finding a good resource, it's usually up to Ray to convince the vendor that he's worth the effort.

Foxy **FACT**

By 2004, small e-merchants—those with fewer than ten employees and less than $3 million in annual sales—may account for as much as 10 percent of the U.S. gross domestic product.

Like many small business owners, Ray has a bit of an inferiority complex. He knows he doesn't have the same kind of purchasing power that a big company has. Transitol certainly doesn't have the same kind of name recognition as a bigger competitor. The people assigned to service him are often not the cream of the crop. He often gets lumped into a large group and ignored. His business doesn't really stand out enough to get attention. Ray usually has to scream very loud to get noticed, and even then he finds that actions are limited. As the little fish in the pond, he gets passed over in favor of his bigger rivals.

Unfortunately, many small business owners get treated this way much of the time. This breeds resentment, wariness, and frustration. Every time a wily fox like Ray enters into a new relationship, he considers whether his business will be treated with the same amount of attention as a much larger competitor. Ask yourself: Do you treat your small business customers like second-class citizens?

Reaching the Small Business Customer

Because small business owners must be generalists, not specialists, they also must rely on outsiders much more than their corporate counterparts. They cannot afford the kind of staffing that a big company can afford. Ray has to outsource many of the functions that a big company usually keeps in house. He has no internal general counsel. He uses an outside payroll service. His trucks get repaired at a local mechanic shop, and his Web site is hosted by a company in Atlanta. Big companies evaluate situations and when it's best to outsource functions they do so. Most small business owners don't have this choice. They have to take the risk that an outsider, who is not under their direct control, will do a lousy job (such as prepare an incorrect tax return), and they will have to pay the penalty. See why the small business owner gets so crazy? He's always looking for people that he can trust to assume responsibilities that he can't do in-house. Are you and your business willing to handle that?

I Mean Now!

It's an indisputable fact that small businesses are more demanding and less patient than their corporate counterparts. They don't have time to wait around. The small business owner is used to getting things accomplished himself and can't cope with delays from others. He does not have the long-term planning capabilities of a larger firm. Everything needs to be done yesterday. He's not used to sick days, two-week vacation periods, departmental birthday parties, or competing with other managers for an employee's time. There are no long lead times. He has bills to be paid this week, and he needs to get a shipment out the door now. When a machine goes down an entire week's orders may go down with it. If the server fails, no one can work at all and things are at a standstill. If a copy machine is not working correctly, there are no other copy machines to substitute for it. Be prepared to deal with crazy, demanding, and impatient customers when you do business in the world of small business owners.

Do As I Say, Not As I Do

For some reason, some small customers have much higher expectations of other small companies than their larger counterparts do. Recently I lost a sale with a very obnoxious fox that complained about our "terrible response time" to his questions. We called him back within an hour of receiving his message. He took his business elsewhere because he didn't have the confidence that my ten-person company "could adequately service his very important needs." Am I missing something? His little company consisted of him, two sales reps, and a warehouse guy.

Big company employees work in an environment where there are controls, procedures, processes, and other people involved in the chain; they know that things take a little bit of time. Many small business customers, because they lack all of these, insist on instantaneous response and attention.

Build Trust

Small business owners crave creativity and a willingness to be flexible. They really need a partner, not just a vendor. Sure,

Ray can be a rogue sometimes, but he can also be very trusting. Small business owners like Ray can be much more loyal than their larger counterparts. They don't have the time to constantly evaluate alternatives. Once they find a good solution they'll tend to stick with it. Unlike larger organizations, they don't have many other companies competing for their business. Mind you, this wily fox is always out looking for a better deal, and if he finds one you could be out on the street. But mostly he just doesn't want any problems, and he doesn't have others in his company evaluating him.

The fox's decisions are driven primarily by cost and competence, not by politics and play-acting. Small business owners like Ray tend not to leave their jobs, so you won't find the constant revolving door that you might at a large company. Vendors aren't continuously re-evaluated by new blood every time there's turnover. A strong relationship with a fox like Ray should normally result in a long commitment. If you do the job for a fair price you're assured of a continuous revenue stream from this customer.

Summary

Have you been convinced yet that doing business in the world of small businesses is very different than operating in the corporate world? Do you agree that a small business owner like Ray is not exactly an individual consumer, but then again he's not a corporate account either? It's an in-between world, but a very large one. There are more than six million businesses in this country that meet the criteria outlined above.

The astute fox like Ray survives through instinct. Many like him fail, and then try again. Ray, like most of his counterparts, would never think of going or returning to the corporate world.

He has limited resources. He juggles a wide array of responsibilities, manage dozens of people and still has time to spend with his family. Small business owners are crafty and imaginative devils. They like it when big companies think that, just because they're small, they're also dumb. Dumb like a fox. They learn when to strike and know when to hold back.

Small companies represent 95 percent of all employers in the United States. These companies are defined as having fewer than 250 employees and most of the companies discussed in this book employ even fewer. Small business owners have significantly fewer resources at their disposal and lack influence with their vendors as compared to much larger companies. Small businesses are little fish in a great pond, wielding a small amount of overall purchasing power, little name recognition and employing people that usually have less of an educational background than those at their larger counterparts. Their existence may easily be crushed by a larger competitor or driven away by an extended economic downturn. It takes a shrewd person to run a successful small business and a shrewd person to sell, service, and profit from one.

Let's talk about how.

The Dating Game

Appreciating the Seven Types of Foxes

The most important strategy in doing business with a small business owner is knowing what particular breed of fox you're dealing with—and how to manage him. This chapter introduces you to the seven types of small business owners that operate in this world.

I devised this list by looking at my current customer list and reflecting on all of the other small business owners that I've met and interviewed over the past fifteen years. There are a lot of commonalities between them. In fact, I was amazed at some of the opportunities that I lost simply because I failed to recognize them as one of the seven types of small business owners early in the game. It should have been obvious.

Don't let this to happen to you. You should be able to walk into a prospective small business and immediately understand what type of wily fox you're dealing with. You should then have no problem coming up with a way to either make him your customer or disqualify him and move on to the next opportunity.

The Fat and Happy Fox

Sometimes small business owners can be very satisfied with their current situation. They may not be interested in taking excessive risks. Greg is one example of a fat and happy fox.

Greg and his wife Janet run JY Machine Parts, a distributor of replacement parts for certain machines used in the plastics industry. Located on a quiet street in a quiet suburb, Greg has operated JY profitably for more than thirty years. Now in his mid-fifties, he and his wife are quite comfortable. They've kept their overhead low and their employee count to fewer than ten. Although they keep their books on a computer, their most prized asset (their inventory of parts) is kept manually. That's Janet's department. Greg keeps the customers happy, provides some service, looks for more parts to sell, and maintains relationships with his vendors. But Janet keeps a watchful eye on the parts inventory. Nothing comes or goes from it without her having some involvement.

Greg's a fat and happy fox. His business is making enough money. He has no aspirations of growing it into a *Fortune* 500 company. He can take his vacations. He can pay for his kids' college education. He's putting money into a retirement plan. Of course, at the beginning, he had quite a few challenging years. But now he's built up a solid repeat customer base and he's careful to keep them happy. He's not going to risk his security with any grand business scheme at this point of his life.

Foxy **TIP**

Your product or service must clearly show an increase in profits so the fat and happy fox will feel even more secure working with your company.

It's not too tough to be fat and happy when you have your own small business. Greg's got no one pushing him. He's comfortable with his earnings, and that's good enough for him and Janet. He has no incentive to take risks. His job isn't on the line. He doesn't have a manager to report to. There is no corporate headquarters that makes demands on his profit and loss. He isn't issued quotas, sales objectives, or earnings requirements. He doesn't have to account for his profitability to anyone but himself and the IRS. There are no shareholders demanding dividends. He doesn't need to issue a quarterly press release. He doesn't have analysts looking at his company. There is no board of directors that is asking for higher earnings per share. Greg's a man on his own. He's fat and happy. He likes it this way. And no one's going to rock his boat. There are a lot of foxes like Greg. So how do you make him happy?

Foxy **FACT**

The top three problems for small businesses are health insurance, federal taxation, and locating qualified employees.

With the fat and happy fox, you should devise a recurring theme and have a lot of patience. I wanted to sell Greg software that would help automate his inventory. But there was no getting around Janet. Inventory was her baby. Unless I could prove there would be major savings, she wasn't about to fix something that wasn't broken. My argument was that with a new inventory system a lot of time could be saved by reducing duplicate data entry and being alerted when inventory levels approached an out-of-stock status. My company gave Greg and Janet an analysis that, without a doubt, showed the savings.

But with a fat and happy small business owner, all the proof in the world isn't going to make him budge until a certain level of pain is reached. So we waited patiently, checking in with him and Janet every few months or so with calls, e-mails, and letters, always reiterating our argument.

And then Janet needed surgery. Nothing serious, thank goodness, but enough to keep her out of work for about six to eight weeks. She was also getting tired of the daily routine. Greg decided to hire an office person to take over some of her duties and stay on afterward so that Janet could do other things. The timing was right to buy our inventory software so that the new person's hours were kept to a minimum and her job was made easier. We made the sale. The fat and happy customer's world was rocked just a little and we had a solution to help him keep the balance.

Be patient with the fat and happy fox. Look for that pressing need. Come up with an argument and keep drumming it in. Use some of the drip marketing techniques we'll describe later in this book. Wait for that event that could threaten his happiness. Provide a solution that increases his financial security. Help him keep that balance.

The Family Fox

Just because she's a good mother and wife doesn't mean that a small business owner can't also be a shrewd operator. But even the wiliest of foxes have families. And for some, their families are extremely important. So they must be important to you as well.

Vanessa is a very successful doctor. She and her partner run a two-office family medical practice in a large city. She has more than 1,000 patients that come to her offices for anything that ails them—from colds to cancer. Vanessa, as a general practitioner, is smart enough to take on patients she can treat and refer those she cannot to the specialists that can help them.

Vanessa is a family fox. She works five days a week and she's on call Saturdays. But her whole life revolves around her two daughters. She matches her office hours with school hours. She almost never misses one of her child's events, no matter how trivial. Besides holding down a full-time job she manages to handle car pools, attend field hockey matches, go to parent-teacher conferences, and get her youngest to violin rehearsal on time. Okay, she can afford a little help. She employs a full-time nanny who, when not helping out with the kids, does double-time in one of her offices answering the phones and doing filing. To Vanessa, her home life and her professional life are one and the same.

Foxy TIP

Your product/service should save the family fox's time. More time saved at work means more time that can be spent with the family.

The family fox has some very unique advantages as a small business owner. Contrary to someone working at a bigger company, the small business owner/family person can create a lifestyle around their children. The typical corporate employee is limited to hanging photos of their children or the occasional drawing in their office cubicle. The resourceful small business owner, like Vanessa, can arrange their work hours entirely around their kids' schedule. She can use her nanny in her office when the kids aren't around. She can have her kids come to work with her all day without fear of upsetting her boss, because she *is* the boss.

Of course, many employees that work at large companies are as devoted to their children as small business owners are. But the small business owner isn't restricted by company policies. She can take off the time she needs without having to answer to anyone. She can bend the rules when she needs to without fear of losing her job. She can take calls throughout the day from her kids without worrying that someone else is listening.

Vanessa could become a much more successful doctor. She could build up her practice to have several office locations. She could spend a lot more time at her job. She could take on many new patients. She could attend more professional meetings, get more certifications, and expand the offerings of her business. She could hire more people and spend more time marketing.

But she's decided not to. To do all of this would require a lot of extra time and effort, and she's decided that any extra time she has will be devoted to her family because that's what's important to her. As a small business owner she's able to make those decisions independently.

When you identify the family fox you should first remember that it's her family, not her business, which takes precedence in her life. Her balance is constantly under fire. She struggles with the demands of both running her own business and spending time with her children. You must prove to her that your company will help her spend more time with her family, not less. Vanessa, for example, was willing to purchase a new accounting system only because it would help her speed up her daily data entry, eliminate duplicate work, and get her get through mountains of regulatory paperwork quicker so that she could leave the office and be at her daughter's violin recital on time.

Accept the family person's lifestyle. Be flexible. Look for common ground. Understand that she's working to live, not living to work. Provide a solution that makes it easier for her to spend more time with her family. Maybe you'll be invited to Thanksgiving dinner!

The Genius in His Own Mind

A few crazy foxes think that they know it all. These are geniuses in their own minds. One such fox is Barney from Information Systems, Inc. Anyone who calls Barney at his office had better reserve at least thirty minutes. Four of these minutes will be to discuss the actual topic at hand, and the remaining twenty-six will be taken up by Barney telling the caller why he's such an expert on this topic, and all other related topics. Barney runs a modest two-person company that does custom software programming. But you wouldn't know that from just talking to him. He's the CEO of the universe!

In Barney's world, he's figured out everything there is to know about business, as well as life in general. No matter that he drives a rented Chevy and works out of his house, Barney's got an opinion on how everybody else runs their business and the mistakes they're making. Barney often regales others with opportunities that got away—the fishing reel company that he could've purchased back in the fifties and made a mint on, or the seating pad manufacturer that he once had part ownership in but then sold it to some jerk who turned it into a multimillion-dollar enterprise. "Just dumb luck, I tell you!" Barney grumbles.

Geniuses in their own minds don't want to *listen* to you. They want to *tell* you. They've been there and done that. They'll always remind you of their vast experience. Barney always begins a conversation with "I've done this a million times already . . ." He likes to hear himself speak. He'll never admit he's wrong—it's always the client's fault, or his employee's fault, or the other guy's fault. Barney doesn't like to read instructions. He doesn't like to be second-guessed. He expects to be treated with respect. He wants it clear that he's no dummy.

Most likely you'll come across a lot more "geniuses" that own small businesses than you will in the corporate world. One reason why is that in the corporate world there are other people there to tell the genius to put a sock in it. In a large corporation, plenty of people will be willing to take on the genius and prove him wrong by the facts alone. There's no way the genius can get away with saying he knows everything when there are others in his company who can easily prove otherwise.

Foxy FACT

The average age of the small business owner is forty-nine years. Plenty of time to become a genius!

But when the genius owns a small business there's no one there to contradict him. Except for the genius's spouse (Marge, Barney's soft-spoken wife, controls Barney like a mother controls a recalcitrant three-year-old), there are few people at a small company who are going to contradict or argue with this kind of fox. Many people own small businesses because they find they can't be a genius anywhere else but in a place where there's no one there to question their limitless knowledge. These crazy foxes, like Barney, have built a cocoon around themselves. They deal with many of the same people every day. They're not challenged by new blood as a manager at a corporation would be. There aren't people vying for their jobs or trying to find a hole in their armor. A clever fox, like Barney, can more easily get away with being a genius and many of them take delight in doing so.

When you need to do business with this type of small business owner you must steel yourself for a lecture. Don't argue with them—that would just be a waste of time. And speaking of time, keep plenty available. Make your answers as short and to the point as possible. Don't ask leading questions. Do not lecture or debate with the "genius." Give him the facts and let him ask his questions. Don't contradict him unless he's assuming something that could really harm him or his business. Let him be the genius. He's never going to change. Show him respect and be very deferential.

Most geniuses are just looking for something that will validate to the world just how darn smart they are. *You* may know that your small business owner is not a genius. But can't you pretend he's one . . . just for today? Maybe he didn't receive the kind of respect he wanted throughout his life. He wants everyone to know that he's no idiot. When a genius feels comfortable that you're not out to question his intelligence, he relaxes and often becomes friendlier. And if your solution is really smart, then he looks really smart and that's what he wants.

So let him talk. Maybe he is a genius. Who knows? Maybe there is something here to be learned. Give him some respect, and don't try to out-genius him. Make things look like his idea. Provide a solution that will legitimately make him look like a genius. But don't expect to take credit for it!

The Micromanager

To be a cunning and successful fox, one must follow the details. But some go a little overboard. Peter owns a fifty-person plumbing service company. He's a typical resourceful, sometimes crazy, and occasionally roguish little fox. And he's also an extremely nice guy—hard working, family-oriented, affable. His employees love him. But they think he's a lunatic, and he drives them absolutely nuts. Poor Peter is afflicted with a terrible disease, an ailment that affects hundreds of thousands of small business owners across the country. Peter is a micromanager, and the road to recovery will be long and hard.

Foxy TIP

Your product/service should eliminate a task the micromanager has to perform so that he can delegate more.

His company bills about $5 million a year, but he's obsessed with the invoice from Staples that says he ordered twenty-five notepads, because he's darned sure his company only received twenty-three. And why is Peter ordering notepads anyway? Can't someone else do this for him? Not according to Peter. He needs a very special kind of notepad and if the order is messed up it could impact the way his people take notes. This is the kind of thing he just must do. He's a wacko about the details.

He also feels he must review the payroll before it's submitted to the payroll service, double-check the math on suppliers' invoices, verify the warehouse manager's count of one and a quarter inch piping, and reconcile timecards to a job cost report. He wants to know why Mr. Jones' leaky toilet took $75 more to fix than was estimated. He signs every check and looks at every expense. He asks his purchasing manager why supplies were brought from a certain vendor instead of another. And he's just obsessed with this recurring warning message that keeps popping up on his office manager's computer, even though he's been told time and again it's not important. He doesn't believe that, and it's driving him craaaaazy!

You're going to find micromanagers at large companies too, but they'll be different than the micromanager fox. At a large company, the micromanager scrutinizes the goings on in his department or area. He can really dig into the details. He can stay focused on his area of responsibility. He can develop a routine for checking the little facts so that the people working for him know in advance that their work will be examined. And the best large companies encourage this. They have the resources to pay the micromanager to spend extra time to really make sure things are correct. At a large company, there's always the need for the micromanager. Some managers are best at sticking to the big picture and rallying the troops to get something done. Still others are better at paying attention to the finer details. A good mix of these types of managers serves the big organization well.

A small business owner like Peter is a different kind of micromanager. He jumps from one issue to another. He's not just overseeing a department; he's responsible for the whole darn company! No one can micromanage so many different areas. But this crazy fox is going to try. One week he's obsessed about purchasing. The next week he's preoccupied with how the jobs are scheduled. And there's that damn warning message on the office manager's computer. It just never goes away. Can't someone do anything about it? You never know what issue's going to be next.

Unlike in a larger company, the small business owner really can't afford to overmicromanage. There just aren't enough resources to make sure that everything goes right. The cleverer fox will often accept a less-than-perfect result if only to keep his business in operation. He doesn't have others in his company who can consider the bigger picture and guide the company toward a vision. That person is him. And he's going to have a tough time leading his people to salvation while inventorying office supplies.

You're going to meet plenty of micromanagers in the small business world. What's more, you won't change their nature. Peter may admit that he's a micromanager. He may talk a good game about building his business, franchising, and opening up other locations. But it's balderdash. He'll never be able to pull this off, not unless he's prepared to work twenty-five hours a day, simply because he's unable to delegate responsibilities.

With this kind of crazy fox, you should gear your products and services to how they'll minimize others' mistakes. Offer him the opportunity to do less micromanaging. Know that he'll never do less micromanaging, but the key is leading him to believe that this is actually going to happen. Speak to his love of minutia and provide answers that help him feel that someone also understands the importance of the miniscule.

To handle the micromanager, you must position yourself as detail-oriented. Share a love of the numbers. Empathize with the needs of doing everything yourself. Offer a solution that helps him be less of a micromanager, but accept that he never will be.

The Lone Fox

The lone fox is the small business owner who carries it all on his shoulders. Charlie started working at his great-uncle's clothing factory when he was only ten. He would come in after school and do odd jobs around the office for a few bucks. As the years went by, Charlie assumed more responsibilities, eventually spending his entire Christmas and summer vacations at the company. As he grew older, Charlie spent most of his time in the factory, along with the other twenty or so workers, cutting materials, working the sewing machines, dyeing, drying, quality testing, packaging, and shipping. By the time he graduated from high school, Charlie had worked in just about every capacity of the business. And he loved it. While the rest of his friends went on to college, Charlie decided to work full-time with his great-uncle and build the business into something significant.

Then his great-uncle got ill. It happened when Charlie was about twenty years old. And though the uncle carried on, he was never really the same. Charlie took on full management responsibilities of the business, and when his great-uncle passed away a few years later, Charlie was fully entrenched as the owner and operator of the factory at a very young age.

Charlie found himself in a plight no different from many other independent foxes. He had no partners. He had no other shareholders. All responsibilities fell on his shoulders. Unlike the corporate manager, there was no one else internally to turn to. Angry customers, late orders, machine breakdowns, tardy employees, government audits . . . all were his problems to deal with alone. He could purchase any help he needed from outside experts, of course. But these consultants, accountants, and attorneys made their hourly fees whether Charlie succeeded or failed. In the end, how much do they really care? The lone fox faces a very solitary world.

The lone fox really needs a partner, but he can't afford one. Charlie would be loath to allow an outsider to take equity in his beloved company unless there were special circumstances. Although the lone fox complains about being alone, he's not anxious to bring in just anyone to help him. So he struggles on.

When you work with the lone fox, you must try to be the partner that he doesn't have. Give him extra time. Don't put the meter on every time he calls. Offer him help even outside your responsibilities, especially when he asks. Try to make his loneliness a little more palatable.

The Unfinished Fox

Some foxes could just use a little polish. "Just call me Freddy, okay?" he said while offering me his large hand that was attached to a muscular, tattooed forearm. Freddy and his brother Alphonso own an industrial motor repair shop in Maryland. The business has been in the family for more than forty years. Their uncle was still involved. In fact, there he was, walking around in his undershirt, the usual cigarette hanging out of his mouth, ignoring us all. The place was alive with activity. Behind Freddy were about ten or fifteen other guys, all perspiring in the un-air-conditioned shop floor, assembling motors, applying grease, drilling, hammering, and cutting strips of metal. Freddy looked at me without expression and said, "So I'm busy, whaddya want?"

Say hello to the unfinished fox. Freddy didn't have a college or a postgrad degree. He worked from 5:00 A.M. to 7:00 P.M. every day, including Saturday. Both he and his brother were supporting families, their wives also holding down jobs, so that they could maintain a decent lifestyle in a decent neighborhood, and their kids could play basketball and soccer. The last time Freddy wore a suit was in church a few years back. He's worked in the shop since he was a kid. He's got permanent dirt under his fingernails.

He's never been to a training class, and the only time he's traveled anywhere was to Virginia Beach with the family.

This fox didn't work his way up through the organization like his corporate counterpart. And who would be his corporate counterpart anyway? A production manager? Maybe, but Freddy also oversees all the billing and collections. He has to evaluate insurance for his employees. And he does other stuff too, things that the MBA corporate employee doesn't.

He's not only required to oversee a job; he's got to first find a customer, price the job accurately so he can make a profit, sell the job, order the materials, produce the job, bill it, and collect it. All without a college degree, professional certification, or corporate training. He's never really learned how to be "professional." No one's ever told him the "right" thing to say. He's never been to any corporate retreats, meetings, events, or trade shows. He doesn't feel very comfortable whenever he must deal with a larger customer. He's wary of others, and he's afraid that they may figure out that he's not as educated as they are.

Foxy **FACT**

Sixty-eight percent of small business owners do not have a college degree.

Freddy's an unfinished fox. He does a great job running the business. But he always wants to do better. He dreams about having a lot of money, and he compares himself to others who do. He's a little self-conscious about his background, his education, and his lack of *savoir-faire*. He's rough around the edges, and he knows it. He wants to be just like the corporate guys, with all the prestige and power. He wants to be able to look any corporate manager in the eye and say, "Me and my high school degree, we're making more money than you!"

Freddy may be a little unfinished, but he's smarter than most of the corporate managers you'll encounter. Who cares about those degrees? This fox knows how to buy and sell. He knows how to produce. He can negotiate and hire and fire with the best of them. Don't let his Tony Soprano-like accent, tattoos, or the undershirt fool you. That's just appearance. Unfinished foxes, when treated with respect, will respond in kind.

When dealing with an unfinished fox, don't hide your background or cover up your own education. The unfinished fox won't hide his. With Freddy, what you see is what you'll get. No pretensions. You should be the same with him. Make him smarter and help smooth out those edges. Offer him a solution that will make him and his company look as good as any of those bigwigs.

The Fox with the Half-Empty Glass

Ever meet one of those smart and successful little foxes that seem like they've got it all, but are never satisfied? This is the fox with the half-empty glass. Klaus is such a person. Compliment his offices and he'll complain about the rent he's paying. Marvel at how he built the travel agency that he started five years ago with his own savings into a profitable six-person operation and he'll grumble about high salaries and excessive taxes. Comment on his high-tech computer system and he'll bring up how much it cost him the last time it went down. The world's out to screw this fox, there's just no two ways about it.

Small business owners are, for the most part, quite optimistic. But a significant percentage of them combine optimism with a sometimes lethal dose of cynicism. There's no question Klaus wouldn't want to be working for someone else. And of course he's secretly pleased that his business has grown and he's become somewhat successful. Looking forward, he does view the big picture as rosy. He wouldn't be in this business if he didn't think it couldn't provide him with a livelihood for many years to come.

Foxy TIP

Always offer a money back guarantee to the glass-is-half-empty fox. This will help temper his lack of faith in human nature.

But that doesn't stop this fox from seeing the glass as half empty. He laments that everything he has achieved has been earned through his own sweat and blood. In his mind, so many others—employees, vendors, the government—are trying to take advantage of him. This makes him a little bitter. It's a cold, hard world out there, according to Klaus. Any number of outside events could topple him. His mottoes: Trust no one. Rely only on yourself. Hunker down.

Now mind you, there are plenty of glass-is-half-empty employees working at larger companies, but it's a different situation. With a negative corporate employee, there will always be others around to help mitigate his attitude. The glass-is-half-empty attitude will reflect a single employee rather than the position of the corporation. In a small business, where the fox IS the corporation, this attitude can easily become the company culture.

The worst thing you can do with a fox like Klaus is to be overly optimistic. Don't think for a minute that a glass-is-half-empty small business owner wants to deal with someone who's bouncing up and down with enthusiasm. Your energy and outlook are really not going to change his tune. It will most likely just annoy him.

When dealing with a fox like Klaus, you need to adjust your personality a little, and try to look at things from his point of view. Don't debate whether life is a half-full or half-empty glass. He thinks it's half-empty, and your job is to help him deal with all the negativity that surrounds him. Accept his position and offer solutions to help him defend against "those who are out to screw" him. Make sure your product legitimately helps him, and prove to him he's not going to be screwed like he expects to be.

Know the Animal You're Dealing With

With most of the crazy and wily foxes described above, you can do business and make a little money. But it's extremely important to recognize the type of small business owner you're dealing with as early as possible. Why? You can cut to the chase quicker.

Remember, you're operating in a world of thin margins and higher volume. You can't dilly-dally around with these crazy foxes. You need to evaluate them as quickly as possible. With experience, you should be able to categorize these small business owners after a short phone conversation. Occasionally, it may require a face-to-face meeting. But, besides learning about them and their business, you should first attempt to associate them with one of the above seven types. Once you've figured them out, you can immediately position yourself to hit their hot buttons.

Unfortunately, there's no list of questions you can rattle off to get the answers you need. You can't just ask someone on the phone whether they completed high school or not. The answer may not even be relevant. One customer may have dropped out of boarding school when he was sixteen, but he still could be a major shareholder in a billion-dollar company founded by his great-grandfather.

Foxy TIP

Remember there are millions of foxes out there. Don't be afraid to disqualify any and move on to others.

Figuring out what type of fox you're dealing with will take some subjective evaluation. At first, you may find it necessary to actually meet the person before you decide. It's only by looking at their appearance and their office, and chatting about their home life, that you're going to be able to get a clear picture. Unfortunately this takes more time, and time is what we're trying to save here. Consider it an investment. If you get really good, you can get the same kind of feel from a twenty-minute phone conversation.

Compare Small Business Owners

The small business marketplace is a great opportunity for analysis. There are millions of crazy foxes out there, and they make up a much broader population than the big company world. If you've been keeping a good database of prospects and customers, it's time to do a little mining.

Do a database dump and take a look at all those foxes you've dealt with over the past few years. Who did you close and whom did you lose? Why? Pick out a few dozen and try to categorize them among the seven types of foxes. Knowing what you know now, would you have approached them any differently? Do you think an alternative approach would've helped you close the deal? Analyze your wins and losses. After you look at the past, think of how you can apply its lessons to the future.

The Dating Game

When we have company meetings, a great topic of conversation is about the clever, crazy, and wily foxes we work with. We love them. And they're certainly entertaining. As I've gotten to know my employees better, I've learned the importance of matching the right employee with the right fox. In the past, I would assign an employee to a customer based on his or her availability or technical skills. Now I've now added another significant factor: his or her ability to deal with the specific type of small business owner as we've identified them.

For example, it would be good to match the family person with an employee who shares the same interests. The micromanager will best work with someone who is very detail-oriented but who can also step back and consider the big picture. The fox with the half-empty glass may be most satisfied (at least, as much as he can be) by working with someone who also views the world in the same manner. Basically, people who have a common background and culture usually work better together than those who don't. So if you have an employee with some rough edges who might be able to connect with that unfinished fox, use the resources that you have. Identifying these foxes early on can help you match your best people to do the job for you.

Summary

One more very important thing to note: It's really not uncommon for a fox to fall into more than one category. In fact, it happens quite a lot. Peter may be a micromanager, but he also highly values his family life and works very hard to balance this with his profession. Charlie suffers from being part of two categories. He's not only a lone fox, but he's also a micromanager! Not only does he not have anyone to delegate work to, or a partner to rely on, but he's also extremely detail-oriented. Because of this, he often ends up working eighteen-hour days, trying to make sure everything is just right.

The good news is that you'll rarely encounter small business owners who fall into more than two categories. This makes it easier to position yourself and your product. It's important to identify which is the dominant characteristic. Charlie is definitely a lone fox, with a side order of micromanagement. Peter is a micromanager with a little bit of the family fox thrown in.

So don't feel like you have to squeeze every small business prospect into some type of narrowly defined category. Quite often you may find yourself using up a couple of categories to accurately describe the wily and wacky fox. There's only so much generalization you can do. Now that we've discussed our seven types of crazy foxes, let's talk about how to get them to notice you.

A Tough Nut to Crack

Getting the Elusive Fox to Notice You in the Crowd

Our "drip" marketing program (which I'll describe in more detail shortly) lured in a wacky ol' fox. Julie called us out of the blue because she was interested in a contact management and Customer Relationship Management (CRM) software application that we sold. She was a fast talker with a hyperactive personality, and she juggled two other phone calls while on the phone with me. She wanted to know every little detail about our product, but she would cut me off in mid-sentence when the information became too much. After I heard a crying baby in the background, she told me that her husband traveled a lot and that her kids often came to the office with her. She said that she didn't like surprises, but she admitted she never fully knew what was going on in her business from one moment to the next. She had so many things on her mind that she would ask a question only to later forget it. Now this was a crazy fox!

Julie had contacted us five years earlier when she was starting up a small business that specialized in floral arrangements for special events like weddings and bar mitzvahs. She was curious about contact management, but that was all. Five years later, she employed twenty-five people and was doing business in six states! Her workdays were now twelve hours long, and her desk was complete chaos. She had been surviving on a little custom-created database, but now she needed to get a true customer relationship and contact management application for her entire company. Oh, and she also mentioned that her custom database had become corrupted and she had a major mailing to do the following week. She was completely manic on the phone, and she needed help.

When Julie had finally made the decision that it was time to buy, our name came first into her mind. She called us as a customer eager to purchase—mostly because she had a problem. "I kept getting your e-mails and your postcards and your mailings and I saved many of them," she later told me. "I knew at some point I would need a system like this and you stayed on my radar."

Foxy **TIP**

It may take up to five years to make a sale. Have a lot of patience and make sure your drip marketing program is for the long term.

How did we get noticed by this crazy fox? Checking her history, I saw that our telemarketer had initially called her four times but was never able to track her down. Following those initial calls, our follow-ups were consistently routine. Because she had shown an interest in one of our contact management and CRM applications, we automatically added her name to our monthly e-mail newsletter list. For the next sixty months, Julie received newsletters, invitations to free training on the Internet, and occasional announcements of new product releases and information.

Even though we never made contact, she did receive two personal e-mails a year from our company, offering any assistance whenever she needed. She was also included in our twice-yearly postcard mailing too. Poor Julie! All she did was innocently ask for a little information about a software product and for the next five years she was sentenced to a stream of communications from a company she hardly knew.

Occasionally she replied (often in the middle of the night) with a brief "thanks for the info" but for the most part we never heard from her. Not once, however, did she ask to be removed from our list, even though she was given ample opportunity to do so.

Foxy **TIP**

A great book on marketing to both small and large businesses is Selling the Invisible *by Harry Beckwith.*

And then one day she called. Why? "Because I'm finally ready to speak with you, and our database has crashed," was her simple answer.

Many conversations, tears, pleas, and tall tales later, we sold her our contact management and CRM application and a few days of service to go along with it. Our marketing worked the way it was supposed to. It dug up the opportunity for us. And when Julie called us in a panic, she already thought well of our organization.

Marketing to foxes like Julie requires a different approach than marketing to larger customers. Getting noticed by them entails following certain rules. It's not an easy task. They are tough nuts to crack! In the world of small business, you need to put the textbooks aside and forget all you've learned about corporate marketing to date. This is drip marketing, and your target is millions of clever, crazy, and wily foxes.

Why Marketing to Small Foxes Is So Different

Some big companies work hard at marketing goods and services to small businesses. American Express targets small companies with special credit cards, programs, and financing services. Banks, in general, like to market their loans and checking accounts to small companies. They understand that these companies are the backbone of their lending practices. Staples, FedEx, Verizon, and Dell Computer all market directly to small companies. These companies understand that marketing to the small business market is not the same as marketing to larger companies. Here are a few significant reasons why.

The One and Only

Big businesses have a lot of employees. Most decisions require the blessing, or at least some input from several people. If one employee brings up a product or service that he or she thinks will benefit the organization, and no one else has heard of this great thing, then that individual is faced with having to remarket the solution internally to get everyone else on board. Of course, product recognition isn't a problem for American Express or Staples. They've got the money to make everyone aware of what they do. But when marketing to larger corporations, you have to make sure you're hitting ALL the people internally who would need to be aware of your offerings. With turnover, relocations, promotions, and reorganizations this is a pretty tough task.

When marketing to small companies, on the other hand, you're only concerned with getting the attention of one person: that crazy little fox who owns the business. Small business owners don't get promoted, relocated, or downsized. A fox like Julie is the queen bee and the primary buyer of everything. She may be running from here to there, but she's still the main target. So even though the total market of small businesses is much larger than the corporate behemoths, you only have to worry about a single person at each company. This will change your marketing approach significantly.

Like Shooting Fish in a Barrel

You've seen the statistics sprinkled throughout this book. Things like "98 percent of businesses in the United States employ less than fifty persons" and "There are over seventeen million small businesses in this country." There are a lot of foxes out there for you to entrap.

Foxy TIP

According to the Small Business Administration, about 800,000 new small firms open up for business every year.

While there are a finite number of big companies, there are seemingly an infinite number of small businesses. In the corporate marketplace, it's not as hard to get yourself noticed by the big company, providing you're ready to pony up the bucks to attract their attention. Advertise in a few select magazines, telemarket to a specific list, and within a reasonable amount of time many big companies get to know your name. The real trick is getting to the right people and then persuading those people that your product or service can truly benefit their organization.

In the small business environment, getting noticed is the biggest part of the battle. There is no list containing "businesses with more than fifty employees." It would go on forever! There are foxes like Julie everywhere, and they're hiding in places you can't even conceive. Some of them make themselves known; others enjoy their privacy. Unless you've got a serious marketing budget, you'll never get your message out to all of them. A good marketing program takes into consideration the sheer enormity of the small business marketplace and stays focused on just the segment that will be most profitable to you and your business.

The Numbers Game

For the numbers-oriented, marketing to our foxes can be a statistical playground. Your campaign may send out mailings to thousands of potential prospects, requiring all sorts of number-crunching. Maybe you'll track these mailings to see who responds. Perhaps you'll keep a close watch on how often these respondents are in touch with your company and how long it takes to close a sale with them. Of course, you'll also be tracking sales dollars so that you can see the actual return on investment of this campaign. If you really have fun with numbers, you can slice these sales down to geographic region and see which group of small business owners from which region of the country responded better to your campaign. Maybe from all this data you can form a more focused and successful campaign in the future.

You can't do this as well in the corporate environment. Instead of thousands of responses you may receive a few dozen, certainly not enough to draw any sound conclusions. Regional considerations, like the example above, may be irrelevant, because the manager who received your mailing in Boston may have forwarded it to a colleague in San Antonio. Sure, you can glean nuggets of information to analyze, but a campaign geared toward the corporate marketplace will not produce the wealth of data you'll find in the small business arena.

Location, Location, Location!

Small business foxes don't like to stray too far from their dens. Big companies have people strewn across the landscape. There are remote sales offices, subsidiaries, divisions, factories, executive offices, etc. Your marketing campaign, directed at the corporation's main address in Chicago, may really need to be pointed toward the facility managers in Chattanooga and Green Bay. Finding the right person at the corporation is tough enough, but this task is compounded by having to find out where that person actually works.

Not so for our intrepid foxes. Julie may be a little wacky, but she isn't crazy enough to spread herself too thin. She can barely keep track of all the orders she currently handles. Most of your small business prospects will have a single location somewhere near where they live. When you market to their business location, there's a high probability that it will be their only location. No searching around will be needed.

Windows of Opportunity

If Julie didn't need a contact management system then she wouldn't have contacted us at all. For small business owners, necessity is the mother of invention. Julie wanted a good sales and marketing system, but the driving force behind her decision was that her custom database went down. If her custom database continued to limp along, we wouldn't have closed the sale.

At a big company, the decision's whether to buy or not to buy is not so open and shut. If Julie was a manager of one group within the company, and she decided that she didn't need a CRM application, the story may not have ended there. That's because at a larger organization there are many more opportunities for your product or service beyond your initial audience. Julie may decide to forward your information to another area of the company that may have the interest.

Things work very differently in the small business market. ABC Company may send Julie at Floral Designs, Inc. a postcard touting the benefits of their industrial floor-cleaning product. However, Julie is satisfied with the over-the-counter brand she uses. The postcard gets tossed and is given no further consideration. She's on to the next disaster. The opportunity is gone.

KISS!

Even our smartest of foxes have their limitations. They can't be experts in everything, although they are often expected to be. That's why they like people to Keep It Short and Simple for them.

Employees at large corporations won't admit it, but they secretly love complexity. Give them technical specifications, manuals, research materials, scientific references, benchmark studies, and industry analysis. Make sure you use all the latest buzzwords. They eat this stuff up! That's because you're talking to a dozen managers and their staff, each of them jockeying for position in the company's political battlefield. These people have the time and are encouraged to read those trade publications, take professional education classes, and attend industry conferences. Their job security is founded in the belief that what they do is so complex and so vital that no one else can replace them.

Foxy TIP

Look at the small companies who already bought your product or service and ask them for a one sentence reason why they bought it. Use this reason in your marketing materials.

The small business owner is usually at the opposite end of the spectrum. Julie is smart enough to understand the complexities, but she barely has enough time to read the back of a cereal box in the morning. She craves information presented to her in the most basic form possible. Her time is limited. She needs the bottom-line facts so she can make a decision as quickly as possible. She's not worried about her job. She's not out to impress anyone with her technical knowledge, especially a prospective salesperson. She wants it simple. Your small business marketing approach has to take the KISS approach into consideration, or you'll lose her business.

Keeping Up with the Joneses

Big companies like to keep up with the Joneses more than small businesses.

Believe me, right now there's some higher-up at one of the big accounting firms trying to find out what the other higher-ups at his competitors are going to pay their new recruits next year. And there's a senior partner at a New York investment house checking out the expansion plans of his crosstown rival. Big companies all know each other. Even the ones that don't compete with each other know each other. Their execs attend the same conferences, deal with the same lawyers and accountants, and have the same kind of compensation issues. It's natural they would want to make sure that they're keeping pace with other companies their size.

So what's the corporate fad this year? Is it some kind of "must have" technology? Is it ISO 9000? Six Sigma training? Reorganization? Mergers? Cost-cutting? Quality? Ethics? United Way participation? Stock option plans? Corporate retreats or special volunteer days? Big companies invent lots of things to keep them busy.

Foxy FACT

In 1999, companies with fewer than twenty employees spent over $30 billion on computer hardware alone.

Small business owners don't have this kind of rivalry. Six Sigma training may be great, but you're not going to find a lot of small business owners enrolled in it. Julie really doesn't care about keeping pace with other small business owners unless it directly affects her. She does care about saving money and improving her business. So if she happens across a colleague who's found a cheaper phone carrier or a better way to deliver product, she'll freak out because she's been spending too much. Keeping up with the latest trends is not first and foremost on the small business owner's mind. Overpaying is.

Marketing to small companies doesn't require using whatever's trendy at that time. Maybe some large company wants to make sure you're in compliance with the new Department of Labor rules before they do business with you. Julie probably won't care. She just wants a problem solved, as cheaply as possible.

And Now . . . the Biggest, Most Important Difference

All of the above comparisons clearly show the differences between marketing to big and small companies. But there's one really huge difference that separates corporations from our small business heroes. It's *when* they buy. Corporations have budgets. They have reporting periods. They employ strategic planning personnel. They monitor depreciating assets. They plan their acquisitions, and they avoid surprises. They consider future purchases. They forecast cash flow and do tax planning. They reserve for contingencies. They like to keep their earnings consistent. In many cases, especially when the numbers are significant, the purchasing cycle begins many months prior to a check being cut.

Crazy foxes, on the other hand, are jumping from one fire to the next. They get surprised. They push their resources to their limit. They hardly ever budget. They don't have to report to the financial community. They don't have contingencies or reserves. They hope that luck will be on their side and that the money will be there to pay. As with Julie, they buy because they *need* to buy.

You can take a long-range marketing approach with the big customer, gearing your efforts toward a planned acquisition date. For your smaller customers, you need to be foremost on their minds so that when their luck runs out, you're the first person they call.

Ten Rules for Marketing to Small Businesses

It should be clear by now that marketing to the small business community requires a different approach than marketing to big business. Besides the differences outlined above, certain marketing techniques seem to play better with prospective mom-and-pop outfits. Here are ten rules for marketing to small companies that have served me well over the years. Some of these rules apply to both big and small companies, but they're critical for knowing how to lure in these tough-to-catch foxes.

Rule #1: You're Always Marketing!

We had been marketing to Julie for years. She had received e-mails, letters, phone calls, and faxes from us before deciding she was ready to buy. The line between marketing and sales became blurred—in fact, all of this work was done by a salesperson. There is sometimes a blur between service and marketing people. After Julie became a client, it was up to the service people to continue to pepper her with e-mails, phone calls, letters, and faxes so that they could proactively keep on top of any issues that needed to be resolved. This helped sell more existing service and discover other sales opportunities.

Both big and small prospects need to be "touched" frequently, in a process known as *drip marketing*. When a prospect hits your database from a trade show, a list, or a referral, you should really have a drip marketing plan in place for continuous follow-ups with the prospect. Don't forget the differences between big companies and foxes that should affect your plan. For example, small business owners will be your main targets, as opposed to the numerous people you must contact when you are prospecting a corporation.

Expect to always be marketing, and understand that there will be a blur between selling and marketing. Your drip marketing plan should continuously touch your prospective foxes in the most efficient way over a long period of time.

Rule #2: The Fox Decides When to Buy, Not You

Julie had been marketed to for five years before she finally decided to buy. This is not surprising. It sometimes takes a long time for the fox to make a decision. This happens frequently in selling to small businesses. A prospect may appear out of nowhere, claiming interest in a product you sell. A cold call, right? However, when you look them up, you find that you've been selling to them for months or even years.

The most important thing is that Julie thought of us first when it came time to purchase. She had decided that she needed what we have to offer. She wasn't arm-twisted into the decision, just nudged into doing the right thing over a long period of time. But in the end it was her decision to buy.

Foxy **FACT**

The average small business has annual sales of $2.3 million—compared to hundreds of millions for larger corporations. For the fox, therefore, every purchase is a significant one.

Foxes are independent and survivors. They don't like to be bossed around. They'll make their decisions when they're ready to make them (unfortunately, most of the time this turns out to be later than it should). Larger corporations may research solutions to a problem long before the problem actually occurs. They know that their current products and systems will eventually fail, and they're in the market now to replace them well before they really need to be replaced.

Your small business marketing should have a consistent message with consistent branding. It should be frequent, not just a one-off postcard or telemarketing call. These foxes sometimes have short memories, so you've got to be foremost on their mind when they decide it's time to buy. And they love their independence. If they wanted to be told what to do, they'd work for somebody else. You can't tell them when to buy, no matter how great your solution is. That decision is up to them. Your job is to be their solution provider when the light bulb goes on.

Rule #3: Foxes Really Love Free Stuff!

When Julie called us, it wasn't just because she wanted a new contact management system for her company. She was in a real jam. Her custom database had gone down and she needed to get a major mailing out the door. She had had it with this system (her employees had been complaining about it for years), and she knew she needed to take a step up. But she also knew that getting a new system wasn't going to happen overnight. She had to fix her existing database to take care of her immediate problem and then replace it shortly thereafter.

When Julie called that day, we did something that was key to luring her in—we gave her something for free. After she told me about her problem, I sent someone out to her office who repaired her database in a couple of hours. I didn't charge her. There was no guarantee that Julie was going to buy anything from us, but helping her out in a jam, and for no charge, cemented the relationship.

Those big company employees always seem awash in free stuff, don't they? T-shirts, golf balls, coupons, mouse pads, coffee cups, bowls of candy, pizza parties, family picnics. Life's a hoot at the big company! Our poor little foxes don't get the same kind of love and care. Sadly, they just can't produce the profits like the big guys, so many vendors ignore them when the goodies are handed out.

Give stuff away to your small business prospects. Make it part of your marketing expense. Give them the odd duffel bag or sweatshirt, or better yet, a few hours of complimentary service or an extra couple of units of an accessory you sell. Giving stuff away, if done correctly, won't diminish the value of what you provide. Instead it will show your commitment as a partner by demonstrating that you're willing to put out a little something for nothing.

Rule #4: Educate, Don't Sell

Julie received e-mails, postcards, letters, faxes, and phone calls from us over a five-year period of time. What were we telling her? Buy our product? Give us your money? No. She received our technical e-mail newsletter, which is primarily targeted to clients. The newsletter has about a dozen tips for using our products more efficiently. It's purely informational. Our other communications to her were in the same vein. Julie knew on her own she could significantly improve her sales and marketing database, but she wasn't quite sure of the specifics. The purpose of our drip marketing materials was to educate her, not jam a sales request down her throat.

Your prospective foxes, intelligent as they are, will not know all that they really should know before they buy your product. Unlike their corporate counterparts, they're not going to have the kind of resources at their disposal to do the necessary research prior to making a decision. Big companies can take it upon themselves to get the education they need. Mom-and-pops will rely on you to educate them.

Make sure your marketing campaign educates the fox. Provide useful information, not commercials. Include white papers, case studies, customer references, outside reading materials, videos, and Web conferences along with your standard product literature. But don't forget to Keep It Short and Simple! You want your fox to be a smarter fox who knows what they're buying. This will make a happier and more trusting customer, and it will help minimize your product returns.

Rule #5: Avoid Slick Marketing Materials

Larger companies expect to see slick marketing materials. Trying to keep up with the Joneses, they like to use such materials themselves for their own marketing, and they assume that everyone else does. When you meet with a larger prospective client, be sure to come armed with a folder bearing the company's logo and stuffed with a glossy brochure, information about your products and services, technical specifications, demo disks, professionally prepared white papers, and case studies.

Foxy FACT

The majority of small businesses in the United States use the Internet for online marketing, while exactly half of small business respondents had implemented e-commerce capabilities of some kind.

Foxes aren't so easily impressed by pretty pictures. In fact, some of them get a little nervous when someone shows up with a lot of high-quality produced marketing materials. "Look at this expensive stuff," the fox thinks. "Maybe this company is going to be too high-priced for me." Small business owners don't care about a lot of slick marketing stuff. Keep your materials professional and to the point, and don't overdo it.

Rule #6: Use Technology

Remember how Julie was constantly hearing from us over a five-year period of time? Well, she wasn't the only one. Of the thousands of small companies in our database, many were getting the same treatment. We used contact management and CRM software (the same programs we sell) in-house to help automate all of these follow-ups; otherwise, we would never be able to nudge so many prospects so frequently.

Such software is extremely affordable (less than $500 per user). There are many contact management/customer relationship management applications on the market today that can automatically handle this type of behind-the-scenes work while you're asleep.

Small business marketing is volume marketing, designed for volume sales. You won't be able to keep track of all of it manually. If you're not using a good contact manager/customer relationship management application to track and automate your marketing, then you should. There are many excellent applications out there, so do your research.

Rule #7: Sell Multiple Products

Ahmed, a fox who owned a small import business, searched the Web for accounting software and came up with our company's name. He e-mailed me for information and I replied back. The drip marketing began! Over the next six months or so, Ahmed and I exchanged e-mails and phone calls. He also received a few mailings too and we added him to our newsletter list.

The problem was Ahmed wasn't sure what he needed. There are many accounting programs available today, all at different price points and with unique features. The good news for us was that we sold four of them. So as we worked with Ahmed, we figured out what his true problems were. If we were only a one-product company, our choices would have been limited, and he may have slipped away.

Your prospective foxes are busy creatures. It's hard to pin them down. But when you finally do, you need to be ready with quick answers to their problems. When you figure out what ails your fox, it's best to have a remedy for them ready to go. Ahmed became our client because we gained his trust through our consistent messaging and seemingly tireless efforts. But no matter how much he liked us, if we didn't have the goods to sell him then we would be out of luck. So maintain a good list of products. Try to have a product or service that meets different price points. Always be ready to offer an alternative solution to the indecisive fox.

Rule #8: It's the Money, Honey!

Many surveys say that small business owners, by a clear majority, prefer quality to price. Where are these crazy foxes? Most, like Julie, are resourceful creatures. They hate to part with their treasures unless they must. Small business owners *have* to be frugal; after all, they're dealing with their very own retirement money each time they make a purchase. The employee at the larger company can buy a million-dollar product and still have their retirement plan in place. At the larger company, it seems that money can always be found somewhere. If push comes to shove, somebody's budget can be tweaked or a request slip can be adjusted to accommodate a little extra dough. Most small business owners don't have those kinds of tricks up their sleeve. The cost of an item is extremely important to them, and their flexibility will most likely be very limited.

Foxy FACT

The average number of employees at a small business declined from 8.3 people in 1995 to 6.1 people in 2000. Crafty foxes are getting more done with fewer people.

When marketing to the small business community, never dance around when discussing pricing. Get it out in the open. Give dollar ranges. You can be a little vague, but let the prospect know that your product costs $5,000, not $50. Your marketing should be designed to get the attention of a lot of small business owners out there, and then filter them down to the right foxes that will be the best customers. By being upfront about your pricing, you can use your marketing campaigns to help you disqualify those foxes that just don't have the budget. Because, with these crazy foxes, it always comes down to money.

Rule #9: KISS Consistently

When it finally came time to buy a good contact management and CRM system, Julie thought of us first because she remembered some of our messages to her. They followed the Keep It Short and Simple rule, and we consistently delivered the same theme.

In Julie's case, we kept reminding her how her current sales and marketing system was costing her money because of lost sales. Our letters were a single page, short and personalized. Our e-mails were limited to no more than two paragraphs. Capital letters, bold print, underlined phrases, and exclamation points were employed. Certain words were always highlighted. It got so that when she saw a communication from us she pretty much knew what it was going to say before she even read it.

This method of marketing is powerful both to small and large businesses. But catching the eye of the busy fox requires a little extra effort. As intelligent as they are, foxes need a simple and consistent message that stands out from the rest of the noise. Small business owners are bombarded all day long by people trying to get their attention, and you're just someone else doing the same thing. Big company employees are often insulated from marketing junk by their own staff, and they can also afford the few extra minutes to read more detail about a potential product or service. Small business owners need the message short, sweet, and to the point.

So Keep It Short and Simple. Think of the theme you want to build. There are probably many great benefits to your product/ service. You need to come up with the one message that you think will get the most attention. Simplify the message so that a six-year-old can understand it. Deliver it in a consistent manner over a long period of time. Keep delivering it, over and over again. Some of those foxes are going to point their nose in the air, smell the scent, and head in your direction.

Rule #10: Word of Mouth Is Like Gold

Bringing in Julie was a lot of work and took a really long time. We had to spend a significant amount of effort sending out those e-mails, letters, and postcards, making those follow-up calls and then checking in, nudging, checking in, nudging . . . until she finally turned into a qualified buyer.

In the end we sold her a five-user software application for $2,500 along with another $3,000 or $4,000 in service. Although spending close to $7,000 is a lot of money for the frugal fox, it's at best a few thousand bucks in profits for the person or company selling to her. You need a lot of Julies to make money, and getting them this way takes a lot of effort.

Whenever a customer gets referred to you, consider it to be gold. Foxes are naturally wary of other predators in their environment. They don't like to deal with strangers. They feel more comfortable dealing with someone who's done business with someone else they know. When a fox is referred to you, their comfort level is that much more relaxed and your credibility level with them is automatically high. It's usually your sale to lose. The same can't be said about corporate referrals that get passed around at golf games.

Foxy FACT

Seventy-three percent of small businesses like to wait until a new product has been proven before buying it.

To encourage referrals, give incentives as part of your marketing program. Foxes are just trying to survive, and they're not thinking about how to grow *your* business. But, all good foxes like a little treat. So help yourself by helping them. Offer discounts, free products, rewards, and prizes for referral business. Remember that foxes love to get stuff for free, so here's an opportunity to get something back. Make a referral marketing program part of your daily marketing.

Summary

You may be reading this chapter and thinking to yourself that these rules are really more sales-oriented than marketing-oriented. Well, consider this definition of marketing: "the act or process of buying and selling in a market." When the fox finally responds to your marketing, that's when the selling really begins. Marketing is the bait. Selling is getting the fox into your trap so you can close.

Marketing isn't just spending millions on brand awareness. Is the person calling you at home during dinner a "telemarketer" or a "telesales" person? When you get an e-mail from Amazon.com with suggested books based on your prior purchases, isn't that the same as a sales call? Is it marketing? When a notice comes from *People* magazine that your subscription is going to run out in two years, but if you renew now you'll save 70 percent, is that marketing or sales? Hard to say. You could call it getting business.

Call it sales, call it marketing, call it whatever. The most important thing to remember is that in order to get noticed in the small business market you have to continuously deliver your message and never give up. You must be relentless. You must never stop. The Radio Advertising Bureau, a marketing trade group, quotes the wisdom of Thomas Smith, a nineteenth century London businessman. According to Mr. Smith, the typical prospect needs to hear from you at least *twenty* times before deciding to buy. He breaks down the attempts as follows:

The first time	When people look at any given ad, they don't even see it.
The second time	They don't notice it.
The third time	They are aware of it.

The fourth time	They have a fleeting sense that they've seen it somewhere.
The fifth time	They actually read the ad.
The sixth time	They thumb their nose at it.
The seventh time	They start to get a little irritated with it.
The eighth time	They start to think, "Here's that confounded ad again."
The ninth time	They start to wonder if they may be missing out on something.
The tenth time	They ask their friends and neighbors if they've tried it.
The eleventh time	They wonder how the company is paying for all the ads.
The twelfth time	They start to think that it must be a good product.
The thirteenth time	They start to feel the product has value.
The fourteenth time	They start to remember wanting a product exactly like it for a long time.
The fifteenth time	They start to yearn for it because they can't afford it.
The sixteenth time	They accept the fact that they will buy it sometime.
The seventeenth time	They make a note to buy it.
The eighteenth time	They curse their poverty for not allowing them to buy it.
The nineteenth time	They count their money very carefully.
The twentieth time	They see the ad, and they respond.

So remember, to crack that nut you've got to keep at it. Marketing is a long-term process, especially to that crazy fox!

The Real McCoy

Disqualifying Scoundrels Before You Take a Loss

The great majority of foxes I know are clever, resourceful, independent, and fun to work with. Most are eccentric, and a few of them are a little crazy. Then there are the scoundrels, like Brad. I should never have done business with him. When I first met Brad I was hungry for work and less inclined to disqualify those foxes that were obviously destined to become headaches.

For starters, his office was a complete mess. I felt a general feeling of gloom from the moment I walked in the door. During our first meeting, I listened as he complained about his customers, his suppliers, his employees, his wife, his kids, and the government. He even made offhand remarks about an employee's race that went beyond basic political incorrectness. He was not a very nice guy.

Moreover, he hardly listened when I, or one of my staff, tried to answer his questions. It was as if he was going through the motions. He really didn't seem to understand what we did, only that he needed someone to fix his computer system in general. He became our client with almost no due diligence on his part. He agreed to purchase our software, but he never signed a formal contract with us. I mistakenly didn't press the point. I did manage to get a deposit check out of him. But then I was forced to pursue him doggedly for the final payment on the product for many months hence.

He was never satisfied with the work we did and rarely had a good thing to say. Like the typical fox with the half-empty glass, he believed that everyone was out to get him and that no one could be trusted. He complained bitterly about every service person our company sent out to him. He made changes to his system without consulting us and then blamed us when things didn't work correctly. He would send me long, rambling e-mails about how my company was terrible, our service was terrible, *I* was terrible. Then he would call me and in a sweet voice ask for more help.

Looking back, I wish I had done things differently. In fact, I should have disqualified him before he ever became a customer. I missed the most important aspect of doing business with small business owners: there's a lot of them out there, and finding the right ones to work with is more profitable than trying to work with them all.

Why Disqualify?

It's very important to disqualify the wrong customer, whether big or small. Too many customers like Brad and your business could have real trouble. A well-known rule in business says that 20 percent of your customers generate 80 percent of the problems. Nowhere is this truer than in the world of small business. Choosing too many wrong customers is a good way to drive your own company into the red.

The good news is that it is much easier to be selective in the small business marketplace than in the corporate environment. A salesperson can afford to be choosier without really risking a lot. My blunder was that I was anxious to bring Brad on as a customer, even while knowing in my gut that he was the wrong kind of customer. At the very same time I was working on a dozen other small deals. So why didn't I disqualify Brad? I wasn't selling a million-dollar product to a limited marketplace. My product was only a few thousand bucks and was of interest to hundreds, possibly thousands of prospects. The beauty of the small business marketplace is that are a lot of prospects to choose from. The real trick is to choose the best ones, and disqualify the rogues.

Foxy **FACT**

Census data show there were 5.7 million firms with employees and 16.5 million one-person businesses without employees in 2000.

One of the key rules of working with small business owners is to work with those you enjoy spending time with, as they will most likely turn out to be good customers. Of course, being a small business owner myself, I'm easily persuaded to follow the money and do business with someone I'm not crazy about if the profits are worth it. But I didn't like Brad from the first time I met him. He was negative, gruff, and untrustworthy. He never looked me in the eye when we spoke. We didn't seem to have anything in common. I could have put all of these factors aside if there were other reasons for doing business with him. But from a personality standpoint, Brad was not the kind of guy I wanted to work with. The more you can "connect" with your customers, the more productive and profitable the business relationship will be.

Luckily, in the small business market you only have to connect with one person: the small business owner. You won't need to foster relationships with multiple decision makers representing layers of management throughout an organization. You only need to be concerned about how much you like the owner (and how much he or she likes you). When you finally do find that small business customer you connect with your chances of long-term success are much, much higher.

Foxy **TIP**

Disqualifying wily foxes in the sales process may become much less important if your product is distributed to mass markets.

The wrong customer can quickly eat into your profit margins. If you're unfortunate enough to fail at the disqualification process your penalties may be severe. Brad's project became unprofitable almost from the start. He stretched out the sales process. He haggled our prices to an extreme. His disorganization caused delays in the installation of the software. His employees were overworked and did not have the time to focus on learning the new application we sold him. We were forced to spend extra (and unbudgeted) time training his staff. We were called in to fix computer problems that were unrelated to the product we sold him, just to keep the ball rolling. Getting paid was another challenge. Brad tried many sneaky payment delay tactics. Unfortunately, he succeeded with enough of them to stretch out payment over many months.

In general, a company that caters to small businesses makes a small amount of profit on each customer. Because of this, there is a very low margin of error, and a small business service or product must be delivered quickly, efficiently, and with as few irregularities as possible. The moment something goes wrong, the profit margin on that customer is at risk. It's inevitable that this will happen with some customers, but the trick is to avoid as many profit-killing delays as possible. Thus, it's important to disqualify those small customers who are destined to be a headache as early as possible.

Doing Due Diligence on the Fox

How do you know which small business customers would be a good fit for you or your business? And how do you make sure you're not disqualifying so many prospective customers that you're hurting your own business? Here are some general rules you can follow during the sales process that will help you minimize those foxes that could potentially be poisonous to your business. You'll never eliminate your share of bad apples completely, but you can work to keep the number low.

Rule #1: Make sure your customer has reasonable expectations

Find out first if your prospective customer has a realistic idea of the results you can deliver. Brad wanted someone to solve all of his technology problems forever—and for virtually nothing. He didn't have a grasp of all the things that can (and do) go wrong with computer systems in general. Being in his own small business vacuum, he didn't have people around him to set him straight. Whenever I see a small business owner drumming his or her fingers on an imaginary keyboard on their desk who says, "I just want to push a few buttons and get my answer!!" I know there's a potential problem.

Rule #2: Trust is essential

A prospective fox must be a straight shooter. With a large customer there are many people involved in a project, all with their own levels of trustworthiness. When working with a small business you are, more often than not, only doing business with one person. If you find that you are not at all partial to your customer's disposition, you need to terminate the relationship sooner rather than later.

Foxy **TIP**

Keep a close eye on how a small business owner treats others around him. Be wary of the fox that is constantly critical of others. You could be the next victim!

Rule #3: Give and demand R-E-S-P-E-C-T

The prospective ssmall business customer should afford you the same respect you show them. With small business owners, you're a partner, not just a vendor. For the relationship to really work, there has to be mutual respect, because your small business customer is going to rely on you more than a larger customer would rely on his vendors. If they don't respect you, then you, your company, and your product will be blamed for every little thing that goes wrong.

Rule #4: Be patient, flexible, and understanding

Selling something to the typical astute fox doesn't always happen according to plan. Small business owners are often much more disorganized than their corporate counterparts. Because many of them are highly risk-averse, they tend to fear change and take a long time to make a decision. Just because a small business owner takes a long time, seems uninterested, procrastinates, or delays a decision doesn't mean he or she should be disqualified. Believe it or not, you actually want those kinds of foxes as your customers. The ones who make snap decisions without really thinking about the consequences tend to cause the most trouble.

Rule #5: Never be afraid to walk away

Sonny owns a twenty-five-person construction company that he's managed for more than twenty years. He's got more than a million dollars in the bank and turns a profit every year. What is his secret of success? He's never afraid to walk away from a job. He would rather not have the work at all than work with the wrong kind of customer. Fortunately for those who work with individuals and small businesses, it's easier to walk away from a small opportunity than a large one.

For a good construction company like his, Sonny finds that there's plenty of nearby work to be done. People are always looking for capable contractors, so he's never short of leads. But Sonny is pretty picky about the jobs he bids on. He evaluates the customer, and, more importantly, he looks at the profit percentage. He considers the project location, the length of the project, and the past payment history of the customer.

Each bid opportunity is put into three piles: one is for those worth serious attention, and another for those that get a strong bid. The third pile goes in the trashcan. Over half of the opportunities that come across his desk don't meet his standards and wind up in the garbage. Another 30 percent are bid high enough to lose, when he knows others will underbid him. He does this to make sure he's not being impolite to those asking for his services.

And there's always the off chance that someone might actually accept his bid and he can make a killing. All other opportunities are bid to compete and hopefully win.

Sonny disqualifies potential customers heavily. He's not afraid if his backlog gets thin. He's got financial resources to cover him through the slow times, and he's confident in his work. Of course, he's not without his problems, and he sometimes makes mistakes. But because of his willingness to walk away from the wrong opportunity, most of his jobs are destined for profitability before they even begin.

Do you have the self-confidence to walk away from an opportunity because you know it's not the right thing to do?

Rule #6: Be yourself and trust your gut

When I met Brad, the fox I described at the beginning of this chapter, I intuitively knew that he was going to be a problem customer. So why didn't I listen to my own gut instinct and either walk away from this guy or lay out my concerns right from the start? I just didn't listen, and I ended up paying the price.

Foxy FACT

Forty-two percent of small business owners are most concerned about making the wrong purchase, not about over- or underbuying.

Small business owners tend to wear a thinner veil of professional pretense than people who work for and represent a much larger company. Most of them appreciate a direct, no-nonsense approach. Being yourself, without pretension, is the best way to discern the true nature of a prospective fox and discover if that customer is going to be a good fit for your company.

Rule #7: Get as much as you can upfront

You'll never be perfect at disqualifying those prospective scalawags. So you must cover your own butt to protect yourself against a potential bad decision. The penalty for bringing on a bad customer is losing money on them, and getting as much cash as you can upfront will help minimize this loss. When evaluating a big company you have the luxury of credit reports, financial research, references, contracts, and agreements. You can also take some comfort in the fact that big companies have more of a reputation at stake and a public image to uphold. Also, individual persons at a large organization are often more concerned with how others view them and don't want to do anything to rock the boat. Many small business owners aren't like this. And the wrong kind of fox can make you pay for it financially.

If you call Microsoft Corporation for a technical support issue, the first thing they'll ask you for is a credit card. They don't want to take the chance that you're a total deadbeat. They want some compensation upfront. Look at your bank statement. Notice those fees that are automatically taken from your account? Don't agree with them? Go ahead and argue—you may just get your money back. But the bank got it first . . . just in case.

Big companies that deal with consumers and small businesses know that getting at least some of their money upfront provides its own sort of disqualification. Once money has been exchanged, a commitment from both parties has formally occurred. A credit card machine? $500. Fees to the credit card company? Exorbitant. Getting your money upfront? Priceless!

Rule #8: Disqualify on price as early as possible

Don't believe all those sales management pundits who teach you to never bring up the price of your product or service until the very end. This may apply to big companies. But singing and dancing around the price is a waste of your and your prospect's time. You may have the greatest product in the world. But if the price is too high the typical fox is probably not going to buy. Why waste everyone's time? Disqualify them early by discussing price right away.

When you first meet with a prospective fox, discuss the price range of your product and services. Always ask if the price range is "in the ballpark" for them. If the answer is affirmative, then you can feel comfortable investing more of your time and move on to other potential disqualifying factors. If you get immediate pushback on price such as, "$10,000 for (insert the name of your product or service)! That's way over my budget!" then you may want to discontinue the conversation at that point, keep in touch with a little drip marketing, and move on.

Sure, you could stick it out in the hopes of persuading, twisting, and coercing. But why waste yours (and your company's) valuable time and resources when there are many more fish to choose from. If you are selling something specific to an industry or to the *Fortune* 1,000 then you may need to be aggressive, but with the size of the small business market it is probably more advantageous to move on until that particular customer is ready to change their mind.

Rule #9: The more "cookie-cutter" the better

Remember Henry Ford's famous line "the customer can have any color he wants as long as it's black"? Ford didn't need to worry about disqualifying his smaller customers, short of making sure they had the ability to pay. His product was the same for everyone, and because of this he was able to sell millions of cars to the masses.

Principle Financial Group sells 401(k) and other employee benefit plans, primarily to small and medium-sized businesses. The company has built a successful business model by taking what was once a fairly complex process of wading through the red tape of filling out forms, getting approvals, and administrating a plan by making it simple for small business owners. The company created a standardized process for accomplishing this frustrating endeavor. That way each small business owner can go through the same set of questions, check off the answer that applies, and within a short time get their plan established. As a result, Principle Financial Group can sell these plans to many small businesses in a cookie-cutter approach.

Small business owners like things simpler than big companies. They can only absorb so much. They don't have the time to be specialists. Wily as they may seem, they need handholding and tender loving care. They don't have the time to be experts, and they don't have internal staff to be experts for them. Coming up with a cookie-cutter, repeatable process is imperative for efficiently doing business in this marketplace.

Ask yourself if you can you produce a product or service that can be duplicated again and again. Can you deliver this product or service to a large number of customers with a manageable risk of return? If so, you've found a great way to disqualify even the shiftiest small business customers from raiding your profitability.

Rule #10: If the ROI isn't crystal clear, then disqualify

I spoke to two clients yesterday. The first was Chuck, the owner of a small packaging manufacturer. He called me in a panic. He had tried to import some information into his database system and something went wrong. His invoicing could not be done. He needed someone from my company to attend to it immediately. At that moment, do you think he cared about the return on investment? "Whatever it takes," he told me, and he meant it. The problem took two days to fix. We sent Chuck an invoice for $2,500 that he happily paid.

Later that same morning I received a call back from Rodney, another client of mine. He's a partner in a consulting company. Rodney and I had been talking about a $3,000 job to upgrade his software partnered with some additional training and support work to make his system run better. He was still on the fence. "I'm not sure it's worth it, Gene," he said to me. "I still need to think about it."

Big companies will invest in the future. They will spend now for something that may not benefit them until years later. They appreciate the benefits of long-term planning. And they have the funds to support this kind of position. The fox will spend money if he absolutely has to. But if it's not an emergency, then you have some work to do. When it's time to sell to a clever fox like Rodney, the first thing you have to prove to them is ROI, or Return on Investment.

Most small business owners have little patience for long-term rewards. It would be tough for me to prove to Rodney that he would get his $3,000 back over the next three years. He wants to see the benefits of what I'm offering immediately. This is different than if you're selling to a larger company. Foxes like Rodney don't have the luxury of waiting for long-term paybacks that a big company may be able to afford.

Foxy FACT

Small businesses spend more than $1 trillion a year on products and services.

Calculating ROI is pretty simple. There are two basic ways to calculate a return—either show the small business owner that your product will increase revenues or show that it will decrease expenses. Compare this benefit to the cost you quoted. It's just math. Keep it simple and verify the return in writing. Make sure to show the money coming back to him in months, not years. ROI for a small business owner should rarely exceed more than twelve months.

Rule #11: Immediately disqualify friends, family, and neighbors

Sonya lives in the next town over from me, and her child and my son once played on the same basketball team together. Although we've never been close, it's not unusual to see her in the neighborhood grocery or at a sporting event. Somehow Sonya became aware of what I do and was very interested in one of the accounting applications my company sells. She asked if I could meet with her and her two partners to demonstrate the software and discuss how it could be implemented. I should have disqualified her right then and there. But I didn't.

Fortunately for Sonya, things went well. Unfortunately for me, I lost my shirt. We spent more time with her than was budgeted.

Her accounting needs were pretty complex, and I felt uncomfortable asking her for more money. I personally invested my own time in her project because she felt more comfortable working directly with me than with others in my company. Because I want to keep Sonya as a friend I've now resigned myself to continue to carry her as a money-losing customer. If Sonya worked for a big corporation I would most likely be insulated from our personal relationship because of the inevitable scrutiny it would have received from others involved in the project. I would have been subject to the company's internal controls and procedures. And I could have blamed the corporation, not her, if things didn't work out.

Working with friends, neighbors, and family is not a good idea. Too many things may go wrong that could cause an embarrassing moment at your kid's next school play. It's difficult to negotiate pricing with a friend or family member—they all expect some kind of a discount even if they don't say so directly. And if there's a problem with your product or service you'll always be expected to absorb the cost, no matter whose fault it is. And although your friend or family member's company may represent a tiny portion of your revenue stream, you're going to feel compelled to place their needs above your other, more important customers, just so there can be peace. If you still want to do something for a friend or neighbor's business, do it for free. Write it off as a marketing expense.

Business dealings with small business owners should always be conducted at arm's length and with as much objectivity as possible. Friends, neighbors, and family members bring too much emotional baggage to the table. If the opportunity arises to work together, politely disqualify them. Move on to that small business customer with no personal ties. You'll feel much more comfortable doing so.

The Worst of the Lot

Besides the preceding rules, there are certain personalities of foxes that should be disqualified immediately—no ifs, ands, or buts. These types of foxes will always be difficult and rarely profitable. Unless there are astronomically big profits at stake, run, don't walk, when you encounter one of these types!

The Talker

This particular fox will keep you on the phone for hours on end with stories, anecdotes, questions, and the like. Sure, they may be nice, but time is money and are you really interested in listening about their kidney stones? You can't waste a lot of time with small business prospects or your sales cost may quickly exceed the value of the deal. Avoid big talkers unless you've got a lot of padding in your time budget.

Foxy **TIP**

The average age of a small business owner is 49.3 years. And the average time he's been running his own show is 17.6 years.

The Nasty Type

It's not fair when someone takes a swipe at you. After all, you're probably just trying to earn a living and help your small business customer at the same time. You may encounter an antagonist at a large company, but they will probably be only one of a few people that you have to deal with. In this market, however, the small business owner will most likely be your one and only contact. A relationship with a nasty type who likes swiping you, your employees, or your products will rarely produce a positive outcome.

The Self-Proclaimed Genius

At a big company there are other people that can bring a know-it-all down to size. With a small business customer you're stuck with him or her. You want to avoid this type of fox for two reasons: 1) they rarely know it all and will tend to second-guess everything you do, which will cause delays and lost money, and 2) in rare cases, they might actually know it all and will soon discover that you don't!

The Old-School Type

We all appreciate people that stick to those old-school values that made our country great. But when you encounter an older small business owner—it's not uncommon to find small business owners who are in their sixties, seventies, or even eighties, and still actively involved in their business—keep the following in mind. A man who has run his business for half a century deserves respect and consideration. Unfortunately, it may also mean that he's prone to be stubborn and highly resistant to change. An "old-school" prospect who's succeeded may be a great customer, as long as you've got the afternoon to spare to listen to his story!

The Slum Dweller

Most large corporations are located in corporate parks or plush downtown office. Because of limited resources, many small businesses exist in not-so-great areas; however, making a sales call should not entail possible bodily harm or a carjacking. You may encounter a small business prospect who operates his business out of the same building his grandfather purchased back in the 1930s, which now happens to be the only building standing in a drug-ridden wasteland straight out of an episode of *Cops*. It's not your problem that he can't get his asking price for the building and doesn't want to pay what it takes to move to that nice industrial park outside of town. Moreover, if your fox is that cheap about where he houses his business, imagine how much he is going to nickel-and-dime you on your product, time, and services.

The Furtive Type

There's rarely a valid reason for a small business owner to be the president, chairman, and chief executive officer of sixteen shell companies all with different post box addresses. If you encounter some elaborate corporate structure, it may well be connected to some illegal scheme. Better to do your homework on what type of business you are getting involved in and, if necessary, steer clear of that fox completely.

The Running-on-a-Shoestring Type

This may sound like common sense but as Mark Twain once said, "Common sense isn't that common." Most small business owners run a tight ship financially. However, if it's very clear that a prospect is having money troubles and running on a shoestring budget, then don't get involved. You don't want to end up being his banker.

Foxy TIP

Don't gang up on the small business owner. If you show up with a team of six people in power suits you'll most likely alienate him or her.

The High-Maintenance Type

If you have a million dollar contract with General Motors, you probably expect them to be high-maintenance. However, a $999 software application, where your profit is less than $200, should engender a different expectation on your part. You don't want this customer demanding the royal treatment or taking up inordinate amounts of your time—unless they pay for additional service. If you encounter a small business prospect who asks way too many questions and spends way too much of your time on a relatively small purchase, you should probably disqualify him.

The Too-Trusting Type

A large company has the resources to research the companies they do business with, follow up on referrals, and do the appropriate due diligence. Small companies don't have the manpower to do this. You should be wary when a small business prospect believes *everything* you say. A little skepticism is healthy, and it at least demonstrates that the prospect is paying attention. Small business owners who take everything you say at face value, with no concerns, will generally come back to you with disappointment in their eyes at a later date.

The Nontrusting Type

A certain degree of skepticism, as mentioned above, is good, but out and out distrust is not. When a prospective small business customer makes it clear that he distrusts the whole world, you're going to have a long road ahead of you to gain his loyalty. This negativity, which will be forced on you and your employees, may or may not be worth your efforts to overcome.

Summary

Disqualifying a potential small business customer is a tough job. When you're in sales, every opportunity is a possible moneymaker. We all like to be optimistic and believe that our relationships will be profitable. It's very difficult to look at a new sale and turn away from it just because your gut tells you to.

But you must disqualify those suspect small business prospects. Select the best ones. It's one of the greatest benefits of operating in this marketplace. Make use of it. Stick to your guns. Be strong. Think long term. Don't focus solely on the lost revenue—think of the increased costs and potential losses that could occur if you make the wrong choice in selecting a client. If the fox doesn't meet your standards then move on. Find another one. Have the self-confidence to reject those prospective foxes that just don't make the cut. There's so many more out there! Don't be afraid!

Oh, by the way, guess who called me the other day? None other than my old friend Brad. He wants to let bygones be bygones and is interested in upgrading his entire system. He'd like to work together again and is talking about spending "a big chunk of change." He hasn't changed, though. He's still a disorganized mess and a rogue. He was already complaining to me about the three other software companies he tried to use, none of which met his standards. He wants to spend a not insignificant amount of money with me and we've been having a slow month . . .

I gave this opportunity a lot of thought and finally decided on the best course of action: I referred old Brad to one of my competitors. It's always good to spread the joy, don't you think?

Poor as a Church Mouse

*Overcoming Ten Common Sales Objections
Used by the Reluctant Fox*

At our first meeting, my customer, Earl, said to me, "Do you realize your father has been trying to get me to see you for the past six years?" I wasn't surprised. Earl was a tricky little fox and catching him was tough!

My dad and I have worked together for more than twelve years. His job is not an enviable one. He spends his days on the phone overcoming objections from the wiliest small business owners. He's not even trying to sell any of our products and services. He's merely attempting to schedule an appointment so I can try to sell our products and services. This is a difficult task, made even tougher because my dad talks to some pretty crafty foxes, not employees at larger companies.

Earl is one such elusive fox. His family business, started by his grandfather, manufactures a line of parts that is used in food processing equipment. He owns a run-down building that is located under a highway right in an urban renewal zone. Inside are twenty-two employees, mainly production workers, who carry parts all the way through cutting, molding, pressing, finishing, quality control, and shipping. Stepping into Earl's offices is like stepping into a time warp. Take away the modern phone system, and you're left with steel-framed desks, dirty windows, poor lighting, and a ragged carpet, all purchased forty years ago.

Like many resourceful foxes, Earl doesn't spend any money unless it really needs to be spent. And a computer system was not high on his list of things that he needed. Small business owners like Earl, as opposed to their corporate counterparts, don't consider purchasing things that are "nice to have" or "*may* improve production." He needs a little more convincing than that before he'll invest in anything.

The problem was that Earl really *did* need a computer system. At the time my dad began speaking with him, he had three women in the office performing accounting and bookkeeping functions. One spent the whole day preparing invoices. Often a quote given to a customer would be rewritten as an order and then rewritten again as an invoice. All of this was being done on a manual typewriter, so similar invoices couldn't be 'cloned' and reused—they had to be retyped from scratch. Customer receivables were kept on manual cards, which had to be checked frequently to stay on top of overdue balances. Open accounts payable vendor invoices were kept in a file cabinet. Checks were manually written from an old "one-write" ledger. Payroll was done by hand. There were no financial statements. There were no real reports for analyzing customers, vendors, purchases, and sales. In short, Earl had a very inefficient internal system.

Over years of telephone conversations, my dad was able to extract all this information from Earl. It was clear that a computer system would save him a significant amount of money. There was no question that Earl would be able to eliminate at least one person from his office. He could put an end to the multiple creation of the same information. He could store information to be reused again and again. He could track open invoices and quotes and orders by pushing a button. He could be alerted when inventory fell below a certain stock, customers became late, or an order was coming due. He would be able to process payables and payroll much faster. He could analyze the profitability of his company each month.

My dad figured that Earl's $25,000 investment for two computers, the software, and support services would save him about $50,000 in his very first year alone. These numbers were pretty irrefutable. He could even finance the amount over a five-year period of time to spread out the cost. And all Earl would have to do to take the first step would be to meet with me and let me explain, face to face, how it would all work. You would think that it was a no-brainer right? Not to Earl.

This crazy fox took his time thinking about this slam-dunk proposal. Six long years, in fact! Finally, he decided to meet with me. Finally, we sold him a computer system. Why did it take this stubborn fox so long to make a decision? What was so difficult to understand about this investment?

For a procrastinating fox like Earl, it really wasn't the investment that was difficult to go along with. It was saying yes. Earl was leery about my dad's bait, and when he finally saw me his apprehensiveness continued for quite a while before he finally accepted our proposal. As a small business owner, Earl had plenty of objections to overcome that we needed to overcome. Some were reasonable, others not. But all of them would make sense only to a small business owner, and not to a prospect working at a much larger company.

Ten Typical Small Business Owner Objections—and How to Overcome Them

When selling to small business owners you need to be prepared for a lot of tricks. Getting a wily fox to say yes is a challenge. When selling to both large and small customers you're going to come across a wide array of objections. There are countless sales books offering advice and tactics on how to overcome these objections and close the sale. Some of these issues are common to both corporate and mom-and-pop prospects alike. But there are certain objections that are used uniquely by these skeptical small business owners.

Foxy TIP

To beat the price objection, try to sell smaller amounts of products or services initially to get your small business customer hooked.

Your job is to recognize the small business owner's unique objection and overcome it. Objections raised by a clever fox are not the same as ones made by prospects at larger companies. They may sound the same, but there's a different meaning. And with this different meaning comes a different response.

Objection #1: "I have no money."

One objection Earl continually made was that he had no money. "I'm strapped," he once complained. "Business is slow and we're working our butts off to keep from laying people off." Other times he blamed his lack of money on taxes due, a big equipment purchase, or an unexpected repair. Of course, he may have been saying anything just to get rid of my dad (it wouldn't have been the first time), but I'm betting that he wasn't. Many small business owners really do get by from hand to mouth. Some weeks they're flush, other weeks they're starving. Having no money is a very common objection you'll face.

A big company employee may say there's no money in the budget. But let's face it: If money is needed, more often than not it can be gotten. There are always reserves, lines of credit, and means of financing for a large corporation. Foxes, on the other hand, often really don't have the money. There is no slush account, probably no line of credit, and financing options are limited. When a big company employee uses this objection, it's usually not because the company doesn't have the money. It's because the company is spending it somewhere else. When you do business with larger corporations, your challenge is figuring out how you can get them to allocate this money to you and away from someone else. Many times you won't have this option with small businesses.

What happens when the cautious fox tells you that he has no money? First of all, you should believe him. It's probably true. But poverty can be overcome. Over the course of your many follow-ups and conversations with him, get him to agree that if he had the money, he would buy your product or service. Work out a payment plan with him. Break down the purchase into phases. Offer financing. Give him terms. We overcame this objection with Earl when we showed him how leasing our system over five years would result in a very nominal monthly payment that he could afford. Of course, Earl still had more tricks up his sleeve.

Objection #2: "It costs too much."

"I don't know. This still seems a lot more than I want to spend." For years, Earl complained that our proposed computer system cost too much money. He wasn't saying he couldn't afford it.

But the price in his mind was still much higher than he expected. For this thrifty fox to purchase a computer system from us, he wasn't going to want to pay what we were initially asking. He wanted to negotiate. The fox cares more about the ultimate cost than his counterpart at a larger corporation. The money would be coming directly out of his account. To Earl, a $50 difference in the price of our computer system meant the same as a dinner out with his wife.

Foxy FACT

Small businesses produce about 50 percent of the U.S. gross domestic product.

When a big company manager says, "It costs too much," the objection is for entirely different reasons. Of course, the manager is responsible on paper for meeting certain goals, operating within budget, and not overpaying for anything. The manager is held accountable to internal profit and loss statements. Certainly, you may hear "it costs too much" from the big company manager as well as the small business owner. But does the manager really care as much as the small business owner? It's not really his money, is it? Can't he just go to some higher-up and get an approval? Wouldn't a couple of competing quotes "satisfy" the "cost issue"? The manager's risk is going over budget. The small business owner's risk is going out of business.

What do you do when the fox objects by saying "It costs too much"? Maybe it does. Maybe your product is not for this fox. Maybe you're selling to the wrong person. But if you're pretty close on price and you're comfortable that you have a qualified buyer, you must either prove to him a tangible, concrete, and quick return on investment or begin your negotiations at a much higher price so you can negotiate down. The smart fox, no matter how much he is in love with your product, just can't stay in business very long by going over budget. The return for cost has to be clear or you don't make the sale.

Foxy **TIP**

Change your own working hours to meet the small business owner's crazy schedule. Be prepared to do business off-hours.

Objection #3: "I don't have time to see you."

Foxes are tough to catch. It's hard to get their interest. Earl has time for no one. Just getting him on the phone is a major pain in the neck. There is no dedicated secretary. Unlike the big company employee, you normally won't be able to get on his calendar by way of his administrative assistant. You probably won't be able to figure out your prospect's routine either. There is none.

Have you found that big company employees always seem to have more time to spare than small business owners? That's because their job responsibilities are narrower. Managers have people reporting in to them, and if they need more people they can lobby for an extra set of hands. Staff from other areas of the company can always help. A manager's daily tasks tend to become more routine and manageable. It's easier for the big company employee to make forward-thinking plans. Individual calendars are shared. Administrative support staff is at hand. Planning is encouraged.

But don't worry. While it's challenging to get the fox's attention, it can be done. The fox can be caught. This wily objection can be thwarted. How? If you call really early in the morning (and I mean really early, like before 7:00 A.M.) or later on in the evening, you will probably catch the fox in his den. Big company employees, unless they're really driven, tend to stick to their typical business-hours schedule. Small business owners spend sleepless nights worrying about their business. Many of them convert these sleepless nights into early morning visits to get a jump on their day and stay ahead of the pack. Whenever my dad called Earl early on in the day he almost always got hold of him. Earl would make the time then if the bait was tempting. Problem solved.

Objection #4: "I don't understand."

When in doubt, foxes play dumb! Of course Earl, like any small business owner, wants what's best for his business. He's no dummy—he understood what a good computer system could do for his company. He just didn't have the time to learn and he wasn't comfortable with the new terminology. Like many experienced foxes, he really doesn't like anything new. If Earl worked at a larger corporation he might be considered negligent because he wasn't giving due consideration to something that could benefit the corporate cause. But at his own company Earl didn't have to worry about the opinions of his staff. And there were no other managers at his level to question his ignorance.

Foxy FACT

Of small firm workers, 53.7 percent had an education of high school degree or less, compared to 44.3 percent of large firm workers.

A big company employee can't use ignorance as the objection. The manager can't get away with "I don't understand." Earl claimed that he really didn't understand computers and therefore didn't think that they would help him in his business. Imagine if a big company employee used this excuse instead of investigating a potentially substantial cost-saving tool for her company. Big company managers use information gleaned from the people who report to them and their fellow managers to stay on top of new developments. There is internal competition combined with political infighting to succeed. This type of environment prods corporate managers to keep up with new things to keep from looking stupid. And if a big company manager wants to understand a new concept then internal resources are available to help do the research.

In this example, our hero was playing it dumb so he could push us off. When a fox says he doesn't understand what you're proposing, he's either telling you he doesn't want to understand, or that he wants to, but doesn't have the time or resources to figure out what you're offering. The fox always has other things on his mind. But as time wore on and Earl looked for ways to reduce his costs, his desire to understand exactly how our computer solution would help him started to increase.

When this happened we had to take the extra time and effort to teach him. We reviewed the software again and again, sent him materials, offered him references, and walked him through certain concepts on the phone. Unlike his corporate counterpart, he couldn't delegate this task to anyone else in his company. He had to learn on his own and we had to help him as best we could.

Objection #5: "I can do this myself, so why do I need you?"

"What? I'm going not going to pay someone to do this for me. I'll do it myself!" Many cost-conscious foxes would rather do things themselves if they can save a few bucks. Earl's no different. He has become skilled at many jobs. He's a survivor. He'll fix the toilet if it saves a plumber's visit. He'll drive one of his trucks rather than paying extra shipping. He'll answer phones all day rather than hiring a temp. It's all about saving money, not about how he looks to others in the company.

So when you propose a product or service to a small business owner a likely objection he may raise is, "Why can't I just do this myself? Why don't I just build my own computers? Why can't I set up my own network? Why can't I design my own computer system? Why do I need you to teach us? Why can't I just read the manuals?"

Imagine walking down a corridor of the headquarters of a large corporation and seeing the vice president of finance kneeled in front of a copy machine, tools laid out on the floor, sleeves rolled up, feverishly working on its repair. Let's say this executive was pretty handy around the house and was quite qualified to fix the copy machine. And darn if it only took him about forty-five minutes to repair everything and save a service visit from the copy company. Would he be applauded by his fellow managers? Was this what he was hired to do? Would others in the company call on him to fix their copy machines in order to save repair costs? Not likely.

To address this objection, use the value of time approach. Ask your small business prospect if he values his time enough to spend it doing things that could be done quicker and better by someone else. We never disputed Earl when he claimed he could do himself what we were proposing. We agreed with him. Short of building the space shuttle, most things can be learned. But it all comes down to time and how you're spending it. My dad persuaded Earl that spending his time with customers was of better use than learning how to build and install a computer system. That job would be better left to us, and Earl eventually agreed.

Objection #6: "How do I know you're not taking advantage of me?"

A small business owner has few defenses against the characters out there that want to take advantage of him—and if he gets shafted he has no funds to fight back. A small business owner must constantly worry who his friends are and who's trying to take advantage of him. And if he makes a mistake he's got no one to blame but himself. His punishment will hit him right in the pocketbook.

Big companies get taken advantage of, just like small companies. But employees at a big company have a lot more tricks at their disposal to defend against the unscrupulous sales person. They've got others in their department who can review a potential transaction and give feedback. They can count on fellow employees from various departments who may be more expert at certain facets of the transaction (for example, the general counsel's office can review the legal documentation or the finance department can review the accounting implications).

Employees at big companies have an arsenal of corporate attorneys and deep pockets in case things get ugly. They've got the resources to investigate, research, and perform whatever due diligence is necessary to satisfy any questions about the pending product or service. And if all this fails, they can write off the loss against a budget and make the case that all resources at their disposal indicated they should make the purchase. The fox has none of this at his disposal. They are out there on their own just trying to survive.

So what can you do to gain the fox's trust and confidence? Not much, at first. You won't be able to immediately overcome this objection. Building trust takes time. Earl needed to see actions, not words. References and written guarantees certainly help. Promises to perform and then get paid go a long way. But in the end Earl still wasn't sure if we were going to screw him, not until we really started to work together and he saw that we did what we said we were going to do. Be honest, perform what you have committed to, and have patience. Over time, this objection will go away.

Objection #7: "Let me think about it."

The clever fox frequently uses the "let me think about it" objection to avoid a decision. Unlike his corporate counterparts, all decisions rest with him. He doesn't have to give excuses or answer to anyone. He can think about it as long as he wants. And often does! Whenever Earl brought up an objection that was satisfactorily countered, his inevitable answer was still, "Let me think about it."

Foxes are often indecisive. Can you blame them? Purchasing decisions are significant. They don't have internal political pressure to buy, like the manager at a large company. They will take action only when action should have been taken months before, Earl continued to spend too much on overhead, despite our pleas otherwise. It was only after a few years, when the economy slowed and he was looking for ways to cut back, that he finally decided to do something about it. Earl has no one to share the blame. He's responsible for the whole thing. So he thinks about it.

Foxy FACT

The market value, or wealth, of small business in the United States grew from $3.4 trillion to $8.3 trillion from 1990 to 2000, but still declined as a percentage of overall business wealth during this period.

At a large company, the decision to purchase a service or product is often not left to just a single individual. Although the ultimate approval may come from the department head or manager, it's usually a group effort. Managers at corporations can share the blame if an acquisition goes awry. And because there are usually multiple people involved it's rare that the decision just sits there in "let me think about it" mode. Someone's going to be pushing it internally.

When a plucky fox like Earl says "Let me think about it," he's secretly telling you that he's still interested in your product or service. It's just that he's still not experiencing enough pain to push him over the edge and make him buy. You need to create a sense of urgency, like a price increase, or a horrific scenario that will occur if your product is not purchased. You need to overcome this objection by making sure your reasons for him buying are clear, the return on investment is obvious (and quick), and you're hammering away the point again and again until the timing is right. After a while, his defenses will fall.

Objection #8: "I'm not interested."

The "I'm not interested" objection presents a pretty big problem to the person trying to sell something to the independent fox. If the owner doesn't care then you've got no one else to go to.

You're dealing with one person here, not multiple departments, and certainly not a purchasing committee. You've got to make the small business owner interested in your product or you're going to have to move on. "I'm not interested" is definitely not the same as "Let me think about it." Where the latter objection is deferring a decision until some day in the future (if at all), the former is shutting the door entirely. A buyer either wants your product or not.

There are many ways to get your product noticed at a large company. If it's good enough, you've got workers, managers, supervisors, vice presidents, and executive vice presidents to persuade. Your product may appeal to a broad range of people across multiple departments or locations of the company. One manager may not be interested but three supervisors may be enthralled by what you're offering. Hearing the "I'm not interested" objection from someone at a larger company may still not shut the door on the process. Someone else at the company may also be interested in your product or service. If Earl had told us at any point of time that he wasn't interested in what we were offering then we would have significantly reduced the follow-up process with him.

Note that you should never remove the prospect from your list (unless he specifically tells you to go away). Just contact him once a year, instead of every other month, in case something in his world changes and his interest becomes peaked. Ask if it's still okay to check in at some later date. Take your notes and move on. The small business universe is so vast that you want to spend your time talking to interested prospects, not convincing uninterested people to become buyers.

Objection #9: "Let me talk to my spouse."

Imagine meeting with a dozen employees at a billion-dollar pharmaceutical giant over a four-month period of time to discuss your product. You hand out literature, answer follow-up questions, send thank-you notes, and call for updates. The employees tell their supervisor how much they want your product. You meet with the supervisor. Then you meet with the district manager. They both like what you're offering. They set you up for a presentation to senior management in the company boardroom. The meeting goes great. You move to close the sale and get the paperwork going when suddenly one of the vice presidents attending leans back in his chair, puts his hands behind his head, and says "This is all well and good, but I'm going to have to check with my wife first. We can't move forward unless she's on board!"

It's never going to happen. But it may . . . when you're selling to a wily fox. Behind many small business owners lurks a spouse. This may be the wife who handles the books, writes the checks, and places the orders. Or it could be the husband who's out on a sales call himself and isn't available. Many small businesses are family businesses. Many foxes consult their spouses on purchasing decisions even if the spouse has no official role in the company. After the years of discussions, meetings, negotiation, and haggling, we had *finally* reached the paperwork stage of the sale when, without warning, Earl pulled another brilliant objection out of his hat. We were introduced to a brand-new person in the process: Emma, Earl's wife. She did the books from home and wanted to know what her crazy husband was doing now. Any final decision would need her final stamp of approval.

What did we do when Earl said to us "Let me talk to my wife about this?" Well, first we kicked ourselves for not finding out about Emma much earlier. When selling to the fox, you must *always* ask if there are any related foxes involved in the company—a spouse, sister, uncle, etc. The presence of a family member significantly changes the process of the sale. We almost lost the sale because of this. Luckily, we immediately went to work convincing Emma. Knowing that without her approval we had no deal, we devoted the appropriate amount of time to get her up to speed on what we were proposing and assure her that we weren't going to take advantage of her husband.

The spouse is an independent sanity checker. We had to get Emma to like us. And we made sure on our next sales endeavor that we struck up a relationship with the spouse much earlier in the game, just so that we wouldn't ever have to hear "Let me to my spouse" again.

Foxy FACT

The industry with the highest concentration of small businesses is construction.

Objection #10: "I know a guy . . ."

"I know a guy who can do this for half the price." "I know a guy who can work with you on this and save me a few bucks." "I know a guy who says what you're charging is way too much." Who is this guy? Where is he and how does he know so many of my prospects?

Big company managers know research. They know facts. They know the competition. They have many colleagues. They know your references. They know people within their organization that have the qualifications you do. They don't just know "a guy." They know their alternatives. They have the time and the resources to figure this all out beforehand.

The fox doesn't have all of this at his disposal. He does, however, have a sixteen-year old nephew who's "a whiz" at computers that's offered to do what we do for a few bucks. He has a neighbor who once worked at an accounting firm that tells him horror stories of all these clients that went down the tubes when they changed their computer systems. He knows the sales clerk at his nearby office superstore who claims that the computer at the front of the store that's on sale this week for $995 will do what we're claiming to do.

When the uncertain fox tells you he "knows a guy," you shouldn't worry. He doesn't trust this guy any more than he trusted you a month ago. If this "guy" was so great, how come he's not working with him already? Unless the business owner is really strapped for cash, or a little dense, he's not going to risk disrupting his business or doing something with an amateur merely to save a few bucks.

You can easily counter the fox's objection by calling his bluff. Offer to partner with the "guy." Suggest that you speak with him because you "really want to hear what he has to say." Be open to recommendations. If there is such a "guy," chances are he doesn't want to be involved either—this is probably not his line of work and he may have made an empty gesture to his friend for friendship's sake. The "guy" may be very relieved to recommend you to his friend as long as you show him a little attention.

Working with the Fox's Objections

Whether you're selling to large or small companies you're going to run into wily objections. How you handle yourself during the sales process may very well determine the success of your sale. And your behavior and attitude must be different when doing business in the small business marketplace. Many of the underlying rules we're about to discuss will apply to both the big and the small sale. But each of these rules must be tailored to the fox because, as we've seen before, he will respond differently and needs to be treated differently than your big company customer.

Foxy **TIP**

Talk to as many small company prospects as you can. Focus on the buyers only. Keep the rest in your marketing pipeline.

Rule #1: Don't spend too much time with an objection

A large company prospect may be negotiating a big contract, so it's worth devoting the time and effort to overcome objections and make the sale. A little fox is rarely going to have the same long-term revenue stream for your business. Sales and marketing expenditures that you invest in the process need to be recouped over the years. Even with my dad's pursuit of Earl, his investment of time was rarely more than an occasional five or ten minutes on the phone. Earl was "warmed up enough" for me to have two productive visits with him and his wife in order to get the sale. If his objections dragged on, forcing us to spend more time than we could afford, we would have had to retreat. In the small business world there are many more Earls out there.

Rule #2: Don't get emotional

Our crazy foxes have a way of pushing buttons that we don't want pushed. It's one thing to deal with a difficult manager from a larger company. No matter how difficult the person, it is easier to hold your temper because the dialogue is more professional and there are probably others at the company that you like and off-set the burden of working with this difficult person. In addition, there are probably more dollars at stake so your tolerance level is raised. But the wacky fox with whom you have to fight every step of the way to get him to spend $99 for your product can very well hit a raw nerve. Don't lose your temper and get emotional. Just because a fox is acting crazy doesn't mean you have to. Step back. Shake your head. Try and laugh at the situation. Move on. There are just too many opportunities with nice and normal foxes waiting out there.

Rule #3: Listen, don't talk, and then ask many questions

Read just about any book on sales and the author will most likely talk about the importance of listening. Listening is a very good practice for sure, but effective listening is even more important in the small business marketplace. In a small company the key source of the critical information is the fox himself. There is no one else. If my dad didn't listen to what Earl was saying during the many years he prospected him then we could have never come up with the appropriate solution. Unlike a larger company, you won't have as many chances to talk to the elusive fox, and you won't have other people to consult. He's it, so when you catch him, listen to him carefully.

One thing Earl really liked about my dad was the respect he received. "People are always talking and not listening." Earl once told me. "They think that because I run a small company I don't know anything and must need their advice. Your dad was one of the first people to give me the respect of hearing me out." Our heroes don't get a lot of chance to vent their problems. Be a good listener, don't talk, then ask lots of questions. It's critical in the small business environment.

Rule #4: Follow up tenaciously

At a larger company, the group of people that you're working with will normally agree on "action items" at the end of each meeting. They'll probably be using some type of corporate calendaring or project management system to assign responsibilities to each other. At the very least it's likely that one person in the group will remember to follow up with you on your proposal, if only to make sure that you're not letting anything fall through the cracks.

Foxy TIP

Keep nudging. You're trying to help the small business owner and he doesn't have the time to realize this (yet).

Earl, like many of the foxes we know, was a different story. If my dad didn't tenaciously follow up with him there would have been no sale. This fox has too many things to remember, let alone returning calls to a sales guy who's proposing to turn his internal accounting system upside down. Always follow up on your fox's objections. Don't let these issues hang or they could be brought up again at just the wrong time.

Rule #5: Know the difference between a rejection and a deferral

When an employee at a larger company raises an objection it may only reflect his opinion. Others at his company may not agree with his objection at all. Further, some objections at larger companies are more similar to deferrals. For example, a very popular objection is that there "isn't enough room in this year's budget." If validated by others then you wouldn't necessarily write off this opportunity. You would most likely defer until the next budget season.

Even so, many corporate buying groups work toward resolution of a purchase. It's usually pretty clear when you've been rejected and there's no overcoming their more serious objections. Most foxes like Earl don't ever make it clear that you've been rejected. Rather, you're just deferred. At some point the decision may be up to you to reject the small business owner. You'll need to decide when procrastination really means no.

Foxy TIP

Think of all possible objections in advance and be prepared to respond to each one. Don't shoot from the hip.

Rule #6: Follow the money

Whereas the big company can raise any number of objections for any number or reasons, the fox's objections will generally be related to money. When this happens you have to ask yourself this question: would this prospect buy my product or service if the price was $1? If the answer is a definite yes, then you know you've really got a price issue (no matter what the fox is telling you) and you're going to have to deal with that. However, the answer is sometimes a little fuzzier.

In Earl's case, if he had been offered the product for $1, his answer would have been yes, with reservations. Putting in a computer system, even for $1, still presented a lot of challenges that this cost-conscious fox would need to understand before saying yes. But there's no question that the price would have made a major difference in our negotiations.

Rule #7: Offer alternatives

Big company people have the time and resources to really think through an opportunity. When they raise objections they may very well be able to address the objections themselves, although they'd like to hear your response too. Most capable foxes don't have the resources to do the research and may not know all the alternatives. When an objection is raised you should always offer a few options.

When Earl wondered how in the world he was going to transfer his history of information into the new computer system, we told him he could hire a temp to do data entry or only enter summary info, which would take a lot less time. This overcame the issue and he ultimately decided on using summary info. Of course, being a good partner also means giving your opinion too. It's nice to offer alternatives to an objection, but a creative fox like Earl may seize the opportunity and use this decision to delay the process even more. So when you give alternatives make sure you also recommend which one you think is best.

Rule #8: Think longer term

Larger corporations practice long-term planning. You may be proposing something that will be purchased or implemented years later. Crazy foxes like Earl are thinking about as long-term as the weekend. He's working in a vacuum most of the time. He doesn't have the time to sit back and analyze like his corporate counterparts.

It's up to you to see the big picture for him. When an objection is raised you should always couch your response in the long-term impact. If Earl has a problem with price then show him how, on an annual basis, the price of what you're proposing is not as significant as he thinks when spread over the life of the product. If he doesn't have the time to think about what you're proposing you should point out to him the long-term impact this kind of procrastination could have on his business. Help your practical fox look further out to the future, and you'll be able to resolve many of the objections he may raise.

Rule #9: Have a very thick skin

At the big corporation an objection may be raised so diplomatically that you may not be entirely sure that it's an objection at all. "We may have a situation that your product is overly compatible with a similar process in effect in the marketing department." Huh? Translated, it means that the marketing department already has a product that does the same thing as what you're selling.

At most small businesses you won't have any doubt when an objection is raised. Given the same scenario a candid fox would say, "We've already got what you're selling, so why am I wasting my time with you?" What he really means is that he's already got what I'm selling and he doesn't want to waste any more time with me! Pretty clear, isn't it? In the fox's world, there's no time to monkey around with words. The fox will cut to the chase, even if the truth hurts. He's not trying to hurt your feelings, just save some time. Put on your thick skin when an objection is raised—it's not a personal attack, just business.

Summary

Employees at big companies look at you as a vendor, not a partner. They've got plenty of "partners" within their own organization to supplement them for what they don't know. From you they want quick service, no headaches, a low price, and a chance to shine in front of their boss because of their great judgment in hiring you.

Our capable foxes don't have all these resources. They're not out to impress their boss. Although he would never admit this straight out, the fox is always looking for someone who he can trust and depend on. He's got so many people letting him down that if he could find that one person who could technically fill a partner role he would jump at the opportunity. No one's saying you should take equity in your fox's business, but when addressing objections take the position that you're his partner, not an adversary. Your credibility will soon go up in his eyes.

Over the years the wily fox Earl tried every objection he could to resist my dad's attempts to help him. He didn't analyze or do any research. Phone call after phone call went unanswered. And when he did pick up the phone he always came up with some new excuse to push my dad off. He gave my dad every opportunity to walk away. But my dad stuck with him. Why? Because my dad didn't view this fox as just another sale. He felt empathy for him. He knew in his heart that what we were offering would genuinely help him. If the situation was different, and Earl was a friend instead of just a sales prospect, my dad would still be recommending our services. My dad considered himself a partner. He conducted himself as someone who has a stake in Earl's success and failure.

And you know what? Over time our wily fox Earl started seeing this too. He accepted that my dad wouldn't just go away. He was genuinely interested in helping. And he started to realize that the advice my dad was giving him made sense. If you take the attitude of partnership with the fearless fox you'll find his objections much easier to overcome.

The Check Is in the Mail

The Wily Fox's Fifteen Classic Payment Delay Tactics

Not only did I get stiffed by Advanced Communications Corporation, but I lost them as a client to boot! Things started out well, but then again they always do. Advanced Communication's owner, a slick fox named John, purchased one of our software products and promised to pay in advance for a block of service time. We invoiced John as agreed and, within a week or two, received his check. Except the check wasn't for the full amount of the invoice. Never mind, I thought to myself, this must have been an oversight. I politely e-mailed him about it and, without waiting for a response, got the work underway.

Guess what happened thirty days later? The full invoice still stood unpaid. This money represented my profit on the job, which was wrapping up. Unfortunately, I was now put in a position of having to ask for my remaining money (which John had promised a month ago). And as luck would have it, John was suddenly difficult to get hold of.

Finally tracking the rascal down, I asked him straight out for payment on his remaining balance. But there was a problem—something had come up with the software just today (imagine the coincidence) and he needed us to address the issue. After much back and forth, I agreed to service the problem as long as a check was sent out. He complied.

Three days later we did receive John's check—except it still was only for half the amount remaining! Aarrgh! A few more calls to John went unanswered, but not for long. As it turned out, John called my office (not me personally) asking for help. As I had the foresight to warn my receptionist to look out for his call, she transferred John to my extension.

Now I was angry. Raising my voice I demanded payment on the open invoice. I threatened. And when that didn't work, I whined. Then I begged. Finally, I cried. And I lost the client. This shrewd fox found someone else to do the service, and I never got my remaining money.

If only I'd been more experienced with these adroit and sneaky delay tactics I'd have been more prepared with my response. After finishing this chapter you'll be prepared with your own tactics so the same thing doesn't happen to you.

The Fox's Payment Delay Tactics

This chapter and the next are about those really devious foxes. The rogues. The scalawags. The rascals. These foxes are not only survivors. They are survivors with other people's money. If you're going to succeed in the world of small business owners, you'll need to be familiar with this kind of fox and the sneaky payment delay tactics he'll use against you.

The wiliest small business owners know that the longer one holds on to the money, the better. However, let me be clear: Most foxes are not unscrupulous, and it's a rare occasion when one will truly try to cheat you out of your money. However, it is not at all uncommon to run into the resourceful independent that wants to hold on to your money just a wee bit longer than he should. Most small business customers have their own system for managing their cash flow, and they like to keep as much in reserve as possible in case there's an emergency.

The reality is that even the nicest of foxes can get sneaky really quick. For example, I remember a point of sale computer system we installed for Sam's Antiques. When I discovered that my invoice for the installation of Sam's system was overdue, I found that that the same sweet guy who told me stories and treated me like a good buddy just a short time ago was now holding back my payment. *Et tu*, my good friend? How could I have misjudged him? When push comes to shove, the small business fox will only be concerned about his own cash flow—and thoroughly disinterested in yours. What kinds of tactics will the sneaky fox use to delay paying you? Read on.

I'm So Disorganized!

With small business owners, you'll find a different approach than in the corporate world. Good luck figuring out how bills are paid! Sam, for example, keeps a checkbook in his back office and some petty cash behind the counter. Most payments have to be approved by him, even if it's just with a nod of the head. If he decides to take a ride in his Corvette, go away for a weekend with a girlfriend, or if he just plain doesn't feel like giving money to vendors on any given day, you may find yourself waiting in line for your check. Because the crafty fox has no strict set of business controls, invoices may get bottlenecked with him. When an open invoice is due it may be preferable to call the fox directly and haggle for payment. The buck stops with him. And because there's little by way of a system of checks and balances, a clever fox can utilize any number of sneaky delay tactics against you.

Tactic #1: The Memory Loss

"Why, yes, I've got your invoice right in front of me. Things have just been so crazy around here recently I plumb forgot. I'll make sure to get something out to you shortly."

This tactic is used when a small business owner lacks certain accounting controls normally found at a larger company. This fox requires a "wake up" call before anything else is done. Sometimes I wonder whether a few of my own clients would ever pay my open invoices without a "wake up call."

Carol is a long time client of mine who, with her younger brother, runs a small manufacturing job shop in Delaware. She often calls on us to provide accounting and computer help for the systems we installed in her business. We frequently receive calls from she and her employees and are expected to respond quickly, which we do. Carol's company spends about $250 per month with us, yet we've never received a check without our asking. Although she is satisfied with our work, and a great referral for prospective clients, Carol requires a monthly "wake up call" to remind her to pay our open bills. I'm told she does this with all vendors, so we don't take it personally. Although it's annoying, we've become used to this system. It's just another little game with a crazy little fox.

Tactic #2: The Missing Document

"Invoice? Oh, geez, your invoice! Y'know, I must have misplaced it somewhere. I just can't seem to find it. Can you send me another copy? How 'bout that game last night, huh?"

Bring up the name of an old girlfriend and our clever friend Sam will have little problem remembering her. Mention a classic baseball game and he could probably recite the entire box score. Ask him how much a certain customer owes and Sam can probably tell you within three dollars off the top of his head. But ask him what happened to the invoice that you mailed to him two weeks ago and suddenly he's dumbfounded. A lack of accounting controls at a small business is fertile breeding ground for the "missing document" tactic.

Foxy **TIP**

In addition to mailing it, fax a copy of your invoice—then call to confirm it's been received.

Brad, a client of mine, runs a small plumbing firm with his father. He is a hard worker, a good plumber, and he cares deeply about his employees and customers. But he pays little attention to details. And he uses this little shortcoming to devious ends. His company has been in the same location since his father founded it and by the looks of some of the paperwork lying around, hasn't been cleaned since. Although in his late thirties, Brad sadly suffers from faulty memory, especially around the time a vendor's invoice is sent to him. I made the mistake of sending an invoice to his attention once a few years back, and I'm pretty sure it's still sitting on his desk right now. Only after numerous phone calls and repeated faxes to his part-time bookkeeper did we eventually get a check.

Tactic #3: The Lost Signature

"What? No signature? I'm outraged, absolutely outraged! Hold on there . . . Sharon! Didn't you look at those checks? Oh, brother. Well, yes, I realize I can void the check and send you another, but I'd

prefer that you return the check to me and I'll sign and return it to you. Regular mail is fine. Take your time."

Sound familiar? Your fox's check finally arrives at your offices but . . . uh-oh, there's no signature on it. Without the right controls in place a cunning fox can use this tactic to keep you waiting for your money even longer. A very effective ploy indeed!

Foxy TIP

To receive your money more quickly, consider credit cards or wire transfers for payment.

Tactic #4: The System Shutdown

"Oh, I have your invoice right here. Why yes, we received all 97 line items on the order but unfortunately there is a problem. You see, on line 86, I noticed that I ordered ten spoons and only received nine. So that's why I've withheld the entire payment on your open invoice. Now, what are you going to do to resolve this?"

Is that fair? It is to the wily fox! When a basic system of controls does not exist, a creative fox can use this weakness to his advantage by subjectively deciding to use one defective piece of an order as a reason to declare "all systems shut down" and hold up payment on an entire invoice.

Take Roy, for example. Before agreeing to a project with us, he and I reviewed version after version of our project plan together, each time with Roy trying to shave a few hours off the project here or there. During our meetings he complained about cash being tight and kept questioning what his responsibilities for payment would be if he thought we didn't deliver as promised (a definite warning sign). Once installed, our project manager made sure the training was completed as planned and that proper support was in place for Roy's questions. Weeks passed as our fox continued to use the system we installed, but no check came. With his invoice over forty-five days outstanding we called to ask what was going on. Apparently, item twelve of our project plan had not been completed to his satisfaction. We had inadvertently designed only five templates for him, and he was waiting for the sixth we had promised. All of the remaining fourteen items had been completed weeks before. The cunning fox held up the entire payment until we satisfactorily completed the twelfth item and of course gave us no advance warning that there was a problem. It took us all of an hour to finish the last template. We received Roy's check a couple of weeks after that. Grrrr!

Why, How Stupid of Me

Besides the four above, there are other delaying tactics that our heroes use, such as playing dumb. The clever fox can make it clear that he doesn't really have the resources or time to fully investigate a new purchase in the same way that a big company can. This perceived lack of knowledge can be used to the fox's advantage when it comes time to paying the bill. For example, a friend of mine was asked to submit a bid on installing a fire protection sprinkler system at our local utility company. During this process, he and other bidders were required to respond to dozens of questions in writing put forth by the utility's own internal engineers and facility management team. He was required to submit numerous references (which were all checked by utility employees), pages of technical specifications, and samples of the equipment he would employ, all for the scrutiny of the evaluating team. By the end of this exercise, the utility could feel comfortably assured that all types of fire protection systems and their service providers had been thoroughly researched. There was little doubt as to what type of fire protection sprinkler system and service provider they would purchase. My friend could only shake his head at the level of inspection he was required to endure. Happily, he got the job.

Unlike a larger company such as this electric utility, our sly friend at Sam's Antiques not only has fewer accounting controls, but also fewer people and resources to perform this kind of due diligence. For the intelligent fox like Sam, this is a good thing. He's free and clear to buy what he wants, work with vendors directly, and pay when he feels like it, without any meddling from other managers and employees that would be imposed on him if he worked at a larger company. There are fewer people involved before, during, and after a sale takes place. This lack of resources can sometimes be advantageous when invoices become due. The conditions are right for a sneaky delay tactic or two (or five more, in this case).

Tactic #5: The Upfront Disclaimer

"Now listen here. You should know right now that if there are any problems, and I mean ANY problems, then I'm not going to pay, okay?"

This is when a rascal like Sam announces upfront that payment will not be made unless he's "completely satisfied" with the product or service to be delivered. By using this tactic, the fox is attempting to put his arbitrary approval on a payment, regardless of little things . . . like the facts, contracts, or legal agreements that would stop a larger company from employing such a tactic.

Rob, the owner of a masonry company decided, after many, many months of deliberation, to purchase a customer relationship management system from us. Ask Rob anything about masonry, masonry supplies, and gutter repair, and he will respond intelligently. Rob has even become somewhat knowledgeable about workmen's compensation insurance and job costing systems as well. But he was very nervous about this new system. Although fairly certain that the software would help his customer service group respond more quickly, as well as track his maintenance and repair work, he wasn't entirely certain.

Foxy **TIP**

Confront the disclaimer head-on and right away. Saying nothing can be perceived as acceptance!

No less than a dozen times at the onset and throughout this project we heard the "upfront disclaimer" from this fox. It wasn't until he was confident that he made the right choice that he stopped trying to find ways to position a sneaky delay tactic. Rob ultimately paid on time, mainly because he was happy with the new system, but also because we made it very clear that an upfront disclaimer was not going to work when it came time to pay his bills.

Tactic #6: The Good Ol' Country Boy

"Well, golly gee willikers, I kinda thought you showed me how this newfangled cash register can give me reports of my beer sales, but darn if it's just not working. Something's wrong with this dang-nabbit thing!"

In order to delay a payment, some resourceful foxes may pretend they're just a "good ol' country boy." They'll complain that the product you sold to them doesn't do what they thought it should be doing and give the impression that they may have been hoodwinked. They'll play it as dumb as Gomer Pyle as long as they can. Why not? Unlike a bigger organization, they've got no one else there to question how true it is. It's just their word against yours. And unless you can dispel their concerns they'll hold back their payment to you, and may refuse to pay altogether.

Foxy **TIP**

Pay a "courtesy call" to the customer right after receipt and make sure the product is satisfactory.

Tactic #7: "Houston, We Have a Problem"

"Why, I'm sure glad you called because something doesn't seem quite right." Or, *"I don't think this thing is working the way it's supposed to."*

Why is it that you only learn of a problem from some of these crazy foxes at about the time your invoice is due? Is this just a coincidence? Is it possible that a pipe that you fixed suddenly sprung a leak just when your customer was about to write you a check? Did the fox just discover the plastic utensils you shipped were the wrong size exactly thirty days after receiving the shipment? Why were you never called earlier about this problem? It's a darn good thing your bookkeeper called that wacky fox about the overdue invoice or you may have never found out about the terrible, terrible difficulty currently experienced with your product or service.

As luck would have it, the dilemma is usually not very significant and can be rectified almost immediately. Phew! Otherwise, who knows how long you would have had to wait for the customer to write you a check, in addition to the sixty days that have now passed since your invoice was first sent. Larger companies have too many people that would encounter and give notice of a problem much earlier in the process.

Foxy TIP

Plan for additional service and build this cost into your price.

Carmen always has a self-deprecating joke when you call him. He's one of those foxes who seem to get along with everyone. His business buys and sells used books, so during the course of the day he does literally hundreds of deals with other used book dealers and publishers. We set up a system for his remote salespeople to track their sales activities both from the office and from their homes. The genial fox seemed pleased with the system, always nodding his head and making favorable comments to our technician.

However, when our invoice came due there was no payment. When we made the call to Carmen he was ready with his reply: "Houston, we have a problem." Apparently Jeff, one of his sales guys in the Midwest, has been unable to connect to the office system for more than two weeks. As we expected, it turned out that it was a minor issue. Jeff changed one of his settings and that's what caused the disconnection. After we spent a few minutes on the phone with Jeff the problem was fixed. Carmen was satisfied and released his check. Why didn't he call two weeks ago? We never got a straight reply to that question. This is just what foxes do. It's in the blood, I guess! Crazy, aren't they?

Tactic #8: The Puppy Dog Eyes

"Hey, it's me, Buck . . . right? Your friend. We've known each other for years. Don't worry, it'll just be a couple of more days and I should be able to get you something. But in the meantime . . ."

It's not hard to fall into a relationship with your foxes, especially those who you've come to know well. So what do you say when he admits a little cash crunch and needs some time to pay down your invoice? He's not some faceless big entity that stirs no emotion in your heart. This is the "puppy dog eyes" tactic, and it's a powerful one, because a fox with good acting skills can shamelessly use it without fear of reprisal from his own management.

I fell for this exact tactic about two years ago when Chris, an old friend from high school, called me for some help. As teenagers, Chris and I spent countless hours together working on the high school yearbook and formed a close relationship that's stayed strong over the years. Now a dentist, my old friend needed a new patient management system installed in his office. Somewhat reluctantly, I agreed to help him do this. The project turned out to be larger than expected as Chris was running a not-so-insubstantial little practice at the time.

Unfortunately, this fox was a better dentist than businessman. Even while working on his new system I could sense the level of disorganization in his office. And sure enough, when it came time to pay my own (heavily discounted) invoices, getting the money from him proved to be an uncomfortable exercise. Because of the periodic cash flow issues brought on by his general lack of controls, Chris frequently flashed me those "puppy dog eyes" and asked if I could just wait a few more weeks for my money because he had other bills coming in. Refusing this kind of a request from a friend is extremely difficult. The "puppy dog eyes" tactic bores right to the soul.

Tactic #9: The "Cash Is King" Ploy

"Look, would you be able to knock a few dollars off the bill if I were to pay you in cash? This way both you and me can do okay and the IRS doesn't even have to know about it" Wink, wink.

A crafty fox sees himself unencumbered by others. He feels comfortable offering to pay you cash in return for a discount or some other incentive, like paying late. By employing this tactic, a fox like Sam could be inferring that you'll take that cash payment and put it into your pocket and thereby not report your invoice to the taxing authorities. Doing this would certainly save you taxes—but then again it could also put you in trouble with the IRS. Is it worth it?

We sold an inventory system to a family-owned hardware store outside of our city. My main contact was the owner's son, a shifty-looking fox named Howard. When our invoice came due no payment was received. I stopped by the store on my way home to inquire about this delay.

With a sideways look around him, Howard tried the "cash is king" tactic. He would pay me in cash if I could give him a few more days. This way, he said, he could keep this capital item off his books and then charge the cash through as something else, under the radar of the IRS. He was also kind enough to advise me that I could put the cash right into my pocket and not declare it either. So now he was offering me free tax advice, too! Putting aside this false wisdom, I hesitantly agreed to his offer, and I took half the cash now and the remainder a week later. For the record, I reported my revenue as required. As for Howard, I was not interested in how he treated the transaction on his books. Luckily the transaction was acceptable to me—if he had asked for a steep discount in return for cash I might not have been as interested, and this sneaky delay tactic could have deferred payment even longer.

Catch Me If You Can

Foxes operate below the financial radar and often make up stories, as they know how difficult it would be to disprove their claims. In a worst-case scenario, the scoundrel always has the option of folding up shop, going on vacation for weeks on end, or generally becoming invisible to his creditors. These options are usually not available to the owner of a larger company. In the small business environment, the crafty fox is able to get away with a few of the following unique and sneaky delay tactics.

Tactic #10: The Disappearing Act

"I'm sorry, Mr. James is (is not) in the office/on the phone/in a meeting/on vacation/out back/with a customer," or *"You have reached Sam's Antiques. No one is here to receive your call. At the sound of the tone . . ."*

If you're a fox who doesn't want to pay a vendor, what can you do? Avoid them! Don't take their calls. Don't respond to their e-mails. Better yet . . . take a vacation! Go away for a week or two—what else can they do but wait for you to return? The accounts payable department at Bristol-Meyers Squibb can't just disappear, but the elusive fox can go underground. Most of them know that it's pretty easy to make themselves and their company invisible if need be. Some may even use this "disappearing act" tactic for quite a while.

Donny, a client of mine from a few years back was an expert at using the disappearing act. He ran a small medical supplies company that continuously teetered on the verge of bankruptcy. As a result, he had vendors, taxing authorities, and other various collection agencies after him all the time. Donny could write a book on the artful use of the "disappearing act." He staggered his hours and never answered the phone. He would leave unexpectedly and return days later without an explanation. Luckily, our services included the operation of his bookkeeping system, so when the time came for our payment we would literally print out our check and pounce on this rascal for a signature the moment he emerged from under his rock. Donny operated in this clandestine manner for many years, eventually selling out to a larger company. I hear he now works for the government.

Tactic #11: The After-the-Fact Financier

"Gee, this looks great, just great. You're really way ahead of schedule. Super. Uh, hey, maybe we can work out some kind of deal between us for what I owe?"

This tactic is a popular ploy because, unlike their larger counterparts, many foxes have less help managing their cash flow and often can't get financing from traditional sources like banks. So the creative fox must devise his own ways to delay your payment while he finances his purchase, and the "after the fact financier" tactic is one of them. Here's how it works: The fox agrees to pay for a project but when the project's done he finds (to no one's surprise) he doesn't have the money. Instead of negotiating the financing for the project upfront like many others, he now finds himself trying to fund the job after the fact . . . and you're the banker! You're not a bank, or an airline, or a phone service company. If you were, you would charge your customer a penalty or additional fee, right?

With Debbie, a partner at a financial services consulting firm, we met the ultimate after-the-fact financier. We made the mistake of believing this crazy fox when she committed to the project, which involved migrating a whole bunch of data from her old legacy database to the new system we sold her. She didn't believe that her legacy data could be extracted from her database and wasn't willing to pay for wasted effort. We proposed the following deal: If we could extract all of the data from her old database into our system, she would go forward with us and she agreed.

We sunk about two weeks worth of time, unpaid, into the project and sure enough, were able to extract every little scrap of information from fifty sample records into our system. We demonstrated our results to Debbie and her entire management team. They were elated that the data could indeed be brought out of their system. When we presented our invoice for the initial eighty hours of work, as agreed, she suddenly became sneaky. She turned into the "after-the-fact financier." She offered only to give us about 50 percent now and the remainder at some future date. The haggling persisted. We eventually caved. What could we do?

Tactic #12: The Poor Little Rich Boy

"It's been a really, really rough couple of months, man. I'm strug-gling here. Business better pick up or I'm history."

The sorrowful fox tells you that your invoice can't be paid because of a cash shortage. You're skeptical, and you should be. Although the data isn't readily available to prove this explanation wrong (like the kind that would be readily accessible on a larger company), this wily fox may very well be playing the "poor little rich boy" to delay your payment.

Drew ran a home heating oil business and always struggled to make ends meet. At least, that's what he always said. This crafty fox operated his five-person company out of a garage-like facility in a run-down industrial park, often dispatching trucks each morning and handling customer service and scheduling calls throughout the day himself. Drew was one of those rascals who never paid his bills unless asked. If you wanted your money you were going to have to go to his offices and trap him. But first you would have to hear his tales of woe, how he had no cash in the bank, and please don't cash his check for three days, etc.

Lucky for me I found one little flaw in Drew's tale of woe. We just happened to live nearby each other, and I would occasionally bump into him driving his convertible BMW or playing golf at a well-known private club in the area. I knew his two daughters went to private school and that he owned a nice vacation home on the Jersey shore. This was all in contrast to the decrepit atmosphere of his business. Drew always seemed to come up with the money for something he wanted—his "poverty" was limited to a select group of vendors.

Tactic #13: The Mousetrap

"Sure, sure. I've got your invoice right here and I've been meaning to get a check out to you, it's been so darn busy y'know? If you can stop by here I'll have it ready."

This is how the fox draws you into his lair, with an enticing promise to pay an overdue bill. And then you find yourself trapped! Desperately seeking to escape with your dignity and a check, you agree to provide more product or service there on the spot. You've been caught in the "mousetrap." Most employees at larger firms do not employ such sneaky tactics as the "mousetrap" because they're not as interested in wringing every bit of product or service from their vendors. Crafty foxes, however, tend to want as much for their money as possible. Some would have no problem using the "mousetrap" to get little extra product or service from you. So watch out!

Remember Sam, from Sam's Antiques? Our great "friend" who suddenly turned cagey when the money came due? Well, he still owes you for that job you did at his shop last month and after he successfully used the "wake-up call" tactic, you may find it tempting to just swing by and pick up your waiting check. Unfortunately, that may be exactly what this fox wants you to do. Sam invites you to stop by, because he says he'd love to see you. Unfortunately, you discover that the real reason he's so anxious for you to drop by is that he's got another leaky toilet in the back and he's hoping to entice you with the prospect of getting paid for last month's work so he can get you to fix the toilet while you're there. Your check is the cheese and Sam's got his "mousetrap" waiting for its prey . . . you. So you fall into it—you're coerced into leaving your office and visiting a customer site to collect your check for services already provided and then wind up providing some extra service . . . gratis.

Tactic #14: One for You, Two for Me

"Our payment policy is 1 percent net 30 on all suppliers' invoices . . . unless, of course, I feel like paying less. Har! Har! Har!"

Some rascals simply take an arbitrary discount on suppliers' invoices when the money gets tight. Arbitrarily not paying an invoice (but paying most of it) puts the onus back on the vendor to collect the rest, and some small foxes gamble that a few of these vendors won't or can't go to the effort to try and collect a small amount. They're right. I've seen many companies shrug and write off small amounts rather than chase them down, because the time they will invest is just too expensive. A practice like this by a larger company could attract unwanted attention.

Foxy TIP

When necessary, change your pricing to customers to absorb any arbitrary "discounts."

Mark, the president of SysteCom has a sinister way of dealing with his vendors. He short pays them by using the "one for you, two for me" tactic. Whenever he can, he pays a few dollars less on a vendor's invoice. He always defended this tactic by saying that it was a "cash discount," but this discount was rarely justified. Now, a few dollars may not seem like much, but after a few months they can really start to add up. In some cases Mark's vendors would go after him for payment, but most of the time the balance would stay there and ultimately be written off. This wily fox saved thousands of dollars every year by employing this sneaky tactic. What's more, most of his vendors kept coming back to him for more business. Mark's "one for you, two for me" tactic didn't make him many friends, but definitely allowed him to stretch and even avoid paying the amounts he owed. What a ploy!

Tactic #15: Back to Basics

If Sam were operating his antique shop in 1784 instead of 2004, things would be very different. Inflation was high back then and the American economy was in its infant stages. No central bank had been established. Currencies from England, Spain, and France were used for trade. Products were scarce in many outlying areas. Many shopkeepers of the day preferred to barter for their goods and services rather than rely on paper that could be potentially worthless. Two hundred and twenty years later, it's still possible to find some resourceful foxes, who when short of cash, like to relive these revolutionary times. Why not delay your payment by proposing an interesting trade instead?

One of our previous software partners became involved with us because of this "back to basics" technique. Years ago, we committed to installing a sales automation software application in their offices over the course of a week. We had seen their document management software and liked it. The owner of the company, Peter, knew that we liked his application and that we could possibly be persuaded to sign up as a reseller. Being a shrewd player, he kept his mouth shut, though, and he let us do the necessary work to get the sales automation system up and running in his offices.

When it came time to collect our money, however, Peter had a different plan. Rather than leaving their offices with a check, we instead left with an agreement to sell their software, along with a waiver of their normal reseller fees, a higher margin, and lots of "free" document management software. Although we never got paid from Peter's company, we did wind up selling some of their software over the next few years.

Sometimes, a sneaky delay tactic can be a blessing in disguise for you, too!

Summary

Because of their unique characteristics, foxes can get away with sneaky payment delay tactics more easily than your corporate customers. There are a few reasons why.

They can blame their payment delay on their own lack of organization. Most large companies have an organized system for paying their bills with long implemented policies and procedures.

They can leverage their own lack of internal controls. Employees at smaller companies wear many hats and are subject to much less supervision than employees at larger companies. This means that more things can fall through the cracks, and the wily fox can conveniently blame their own lack of internal controls for not making payment.

Fewer people are involved in the payment approval process. If there is a problem with your product or service at a larger customer there would be many people who would raise the red flag. It would be much tougher for any one employee to play sneaky payment delay games without raising an eyebrow or two from his or her colleagues.

An employee at a larger company gets her paycheck each week whether or not your invoice gets paid. This may seem like little motivation to pay you. But conversely, the longer a fox stretches out his payments to his customers, the more money remains in his account. There's a lot more motivation for the wily fox to delay payment than his counterpart at a larger organization.

These fifteen sneaky tactics are by no means a comprehensive list. There are more. But keeping your eyes open for these kinds of tricks will help you to not make the same kind of mistake I made with Advanced Communications Corporation. If I had the brains to realize that John was trying on a few of these schemes I would have been able to take a deep breath and utilize some of the tactics I outline in the next chapter to thwart his efforts. Instead, I just got angry and, because of my ignorance, not only lost this small business customer but his remaining balance forever.

You're never going to know when a sneaky payment delay tactic is going to be pulled on you. Even the nicest small business customer may turn out to be a rogue when the time for payment is due. The trick is to not make the same mistake twice. When a wily fox shows the tendency to use a sneaky delay tactic or two, your guard must be up for all future transactions. The counter-tactics should be applied only to those rascals that have proven their deviousness in the past.

For every sneaky delay tactic pulled by the small business owner, there's a counter-tactic. But there are also many things you can do to avoid, as well as thwart, future sneaky payment delays. We'll look at some of these maneuvers in the next chapter.

No Defense Like a Good Offense

Proven Strategies to Get Your Money from a Rascally Fox

Mitch, President of Equipment Fabricators, had a big problem. His company, a forty-employee manufacturer of equipment used in the plastics industry, used one of our customer relationship management database products. However, the product was an outdated version and some of the hardware it relied on was failing. Data was being lost. Employees were getting frustrated. Sales were being affected. Things were deteriorating quickly. Finally, one fateful Tuesday, everything blew up. The corruption in his database was so bad that no one could work. Sales activity came to a halt. Mitch called me in a panic. "We've got to do something now!!" he said. "Can you please help?!"

Equipment Fabricators was a very good client of ours. We had done a lot of work for them in the past and I knew there was a lot more to come. So we sprang into action. I cleared the schedules of a couple of our very best technicians. We first performed the necessary fixes to get his application back up and running. Then, over the next two weeks, we supervised the repair of his hardware, upgraded his software and performed a database clean up for his entire system. When the smoke cleared the company was working smoothly again. Mitch was pleased. We sent our bill for the time incurred.

Now, Mitch is a different kind of fox. He was crafty, but he didn't play any sneaky payment delay tactics. In fact, he called me shortly after our invoice made it to his desk. He told me he would definitely pay our invoice within the week and he was a man of his word. I did receive Mitch's check a week later. But of course that wasn't the reason for his call.

The reason for Mitch's call was that he didn't want to pay the full amount on the invoice. Was the service bad? No. Was it not timely? Not at all. Did my people do poor work? Nope. Then why didn't he want to pay the full invoice amount? Because it was just too expensive. That was the real reason he called.

Of course, Mitch didn't come right out and say this. That argument wouldn't fly very well, especially after all the hard work we had just done for him. Instead, he said he called me because he wanted to "understand" why the hours were more than he expected. He wanted to "explore" ways to address this "issue." He wanted to "discuss" whether the time was spent as "efficiently" as it could have been. When a fox calls me to discuss an invoice, it's never, ever because the invoice was too low. Mitch was no different.

You had to admire him though. He watched every penny that leaves his bank account. Like many of the experienced foxes we did business with, he'd take a chance on saving a few bucks . . . just by asking. And in my case he had me cornered. He was still (at that time) sitting on my open invoice. He was a good client. There was definitely more work on the horizon. And he got to me personally—being a small business owner myself, I understand what it feels like to get unexpected sticker shock. And Mitch could innocently make his request. He's crazy like a fox!

So I caved. I offered him 10 percent off the invoice for no reason other than he asked. And he took it gleefully. What was I going to do, argue with him? Spend even more of my time haggling? Potentially upset a good customer by saying the wrong thing? We performed a great service, at a moment's notice, for a longtime client. We saved him countless hours of lost time and productivity. We saved his business potentially thousands in lost sales. And it cost me. The wily fox scored one.

But is that the end of the story? Did I roll over and play dead? Thank goodness, no. I've learned a few tricks myself over the past fifteen years. If we were at fault in any way I would have had no issue refunding Mitch a few bucks. But in this case, like so many others, we had to settle for less for no other reason than to keep the customer and even protect our ability to get paid. After getting my check from Equipment Fabricators (less the 10 percent discount) I made a few offensive moves of my own. Over the next six months I got back the 10 percent, plus a lot more. What did I do? I employed a few time-tested strategies for getting paid from these wily small business owners. I kept the client, and I made a profit from him. Here's what to do if you want to succeed with the fox.

Why Getting Your Money from a Wily Fox Is Such a Pain

In the previous chapter we discussed the tactics a rascal can employ to avoid or delay payment to a vendor. This chapter will offer some ways to handle the problem. When you perform a service or sell a product to a larger company, you will most likely get paid with minimal aggravation or delay tactics. However, perform a service or sell the exact same product to a small business, and more often than not you will have to fight for your money. Why is it so much more difficult to collect money from a small business owner than a larger company? Here are a few reasons.

Foxy TIP

Notice early on if a small business owner is disorganized. Change your collection tactics to thwart this potential excuse.

A Greater Chance of Mismanagement

Big companies have managers. Each manager is responsible for his or her area of the company, be it sales, personnel, operations, or finance. Managers supervise people in their departments, and they are usually supervised by executives above them. Management at a big company usually implements internal controls. They make sure that there are rules to follow. They have policies and procedures to support these rules. This doesn't mean that big companies are never mismanaged. They sometimes are. However, at a small company the business owner is responsible for all decisions and there is a much greater chance that he is going to make a mistake. He has no safety net of other people to help him. He's responsible for it all. When a small business owner, like Mitch, makes a mistake (not paying attention to the hours we spent on his project) it will usually impact his cash flow. And when cash flow gets interrupted his vendors will feel the effects. When you do business in the small business environment you must keep a close eye on your open invoices in case your customer's mismanagement results in your own cash flow problems.

He's Got Moxie

You have to admire Mitch, don't you? He's got moxie. Guts. Chutzpah. He lost no sleep over calling up and asking for a discount on an invoice, knowing full well there was no real reason for a discount. If he had the opportunity he'd do the same with anyone, no matter how big or small. If a small business owner like Mitch can save a few bucks just by asking, he definitely will. He's not afraid to embarrass himself in the process. You're not going to find many people in a big company who possess that kind of moxie.

Most corporate employees don't really care as much about saving a few bucks. It's certainly not going back into their pockets. A typical big company employee wouldn't want to make himself look foolish, or make an unreasonable request for a discount. What happens if the vendor complains back to his boss? What if it reflects poorly on his company? Generally speaking, it's not in the fox's best interest to care too much about what other people think about them, especially vendors. If the small business owner can save a few bucks simply by asking, no matter how bold the question might be, many of them will.

He's Been Taken Advantage Of

Henry is in his early sixties and operates a declining theatre ticket agency in a rundown part of the city. Every day for him is a struggle, and he wants nothing more than to sell his business and retire. Unfortunately, there are no buyers and his kids aren't interested in carrying on the family tradition. Every day Henry deals with characters trying to take advantage of him. His employees often show up late, if at all. His vendors sometimes ship him lousy product or overcharge him. The city thinks up new fees and taxes to impose on him. And his customers play sneaky delay tactics with him all the time. When it's time for my company to collect our invoice this crazy fox is not so anxious to pay.

It's not like we didn't do a good job for him, either; it's just that he's got a long line of other people waiting for money from him. And because Henry has been screwed before he's grown a thick skin over the years. He doesn't have a lot of guilt about hanging me out to dry. When we call for payment, he grumbles into the phone, "You'll get your money, you'll get your money." Like it's our fault for asking! He's been around long enough to know that he'll eventually pay what he owes (or most of it). But if a vendor like me has to wait an extra month or so, that's the way it is. Corporate management is concerned about their company's reputation and standing among its vendors and the business community. Some foxes that have been screwed before have no problem screwing someone else if it helps cash flow. Keep this in mind well before your invoice's thirty days are up.

He Can Be Tough to Find

One more thing about Henry: he likes to play the Disappearing Act a lot. Many of these rogues do this quite often when money is owed—it's a classic sneaky delaying tactic. This makes getting payment from this kind of small business owner a lot harder than from a big company. If there's a problem getting your money from a larger company, there are lots of people you can call. You've got your choice of accounts payable, customer service, accounting, finance, even executive management. But in the world of small business, it's Henry and no one else but Henry who has the answers. And if you can't track him down, you're not going to get paid. It's helpful to learn his habits early on, just in case you need to find him in the future.

You May Feel Sympathy

When WorldCom went bust you probably didn't see a whole lot of people crying for their management. The partners at Arthur Anderson, one of the five biggest accounting firms in the world, watched in horror as their venerable firm went down in flames in just a few months, while their so-called peers in the industry ruthlessly snatched up their clients and employees without remorse. But when a local pizza shop in my neighborhood recently closed its doors the entire community was up in arms. When a longtime supplier of metal sheeting couldn't make ends meet, its customers and suppliers both felt sad for its owners. When a family-owned tool and die manufacturer went bankrupt, everyone who learned about its demise was saddened.

It's easier to feel sympathetic for a small business owner's plight compared to a corporation's. Maybe it's because every small business owner who goes under represents a defeat of a little piece of the American dream. When an invoice is due from a struggling little company it's natural to bend a little and see what one can do to help out the situation. When that same invoice is due from WorldCom the first thing you do is call your attorney to be part of the liquidation settlement. Be wary of this sympathetic nature. Some of these scoundrels know it and will take advantage.

It's His Money, Not Someone Else's

Always remember that for the fox, it's personal. The minute Henry pays a vendor what is owed them the money leaves his account. His. Not the company's account. Henry's account. That's why he takes getting screwed more to heart. Mitch will make the bold move of calling and asking for a discount because Mitch wants to keep his money in his account. When business becomes personal, the rules change.

Don't you think an accounts payable clerk at Big Company, Inc. would be tougher to deal with if she knew that the money being paid was coming out of her own checking account? Of course she would be. But because it isn't she can be objective about managing accounts payable because to her it's all funny money anyway. To her these are just numbers on a report that have no impact on her own personal finances. For the independent fox, the situation is the exact opposite. These are not make-believe figures. It's the owner's mortgage payment, tuition bill, and vacation money. It's natural for the fox to not want to part with this money so readily, even when it's the right thing to do. So remember that when doing business with these wily foxes, money is personal.

Strategies to Use Before You Make the Initial Sale

A cunning fox may employ lots of sneaky tactics to avoid paying his customers. But this doesn't mean that you have to fall victim to these tactics. There are lots of things you can do to counter these little wily devices, even before you've made the initial sale.

Get Credit Indemnity Insurance

When you have to hire a collection agency, you know that you've played out all of your cards. Have you ever worked with a factoring firm? These types of companies buy your open invoices for eighty or ninety cents on the dollar and then collect payment directly from your customers. Although they're a great boost to cash flow, by using a firm such as this you are compromising most of your profit and are instead merely settling for a reimbursement of your costs. There's an even better solution: Before you make the sale, get credit indemnity insurance. It's a great hedge against the sneaky delay tactic. Terry, a partner at one of my customers, did this to protect his firm against his small business customers. It worked like a charm. Terry submitted a list of his customers in advance to the credit insurance company with proposed credit lines. The insurance company did credit checks and approved the list.

Foxy TIP

Use popular Internet search engines like Yahoo! and Google to find credit indemnity insurance companies. Don't forget to always get references.

Any time a sneaky delay tactic was attempted, Terry turned the invoice over to the insurance company and was immediately paid. The insurance company then forwarded the invoice to their own internal collection department for further processing. Terry pays an annual premium for this service, which is calculated as a percentage of his total sales. Not only does he collect on invoices, which previously went unpaid, he spends a lot less time chasing down money—which has cost associated with it as well. In the small business world, where there are smaller dollar amounts and crazy foxes, credit indemnity insurance is a great thing to consider.

Use Good Technology

You're going to have lots of these scalawags to pursue, more so than if you were dealing with a few large companies. So before you make a sale, consider buying and installing a good contact management program. Investing in a popular contact management software programs for as little as $500 can help avoid overdue invoices before they become overdue. Most applications available today allow the user to set up friendly, but firm, e-mail and fax templates, customized for each of your customers and then schedule those documents to be sent again and again as often as you like.

In addition to generating documents you can schedule recurring follow-ups to keep the pressure on. If a fox needs a "wake-up call," then oblige him by providing many over the course of a few weeks so that he has little reason to forget about your invoice. There's also some great software, readily available, which will monitor your own accounting system and automatically alert you to any overdue, or potentially overdue, invoices so you can take pre-emptive action.

Accept That Legal Options Are Limited

When you first fall victim to the "one for you, two for me" tactic, your initial reaction may be to hire an attorney and go after the customer. You may feel the same way when another rascal tries the "poor little rich boy" scheme. However, you should take a minute to realize that a sneaky delay tactic is just that—an excuse for buying a little time. Rarely do customers that employ sneaky delay tactics turn into actual bad debts. Most of the time these foxes are using you as a means of financing their other debts; eventually, when your turn comes, you'll get paid.

A sneaky delay tactic isn't usually breaking any laws. Centuries ago, nonpayment of debts could result in jail—or even death—to the debtor. Nowadays, the laws actually favor him. For example, did you know that if you receive a credit card payment from a small customer he's entitled to a refund for at least ninety days afterward? And if he applies for the refund from your credit card company then the money is *automatically* taken from your account and put into escrow, no questions asked? Other than writing a few nasty letters, there's little else an attorney can do. Fortunately, there is little reason to ever involve a lawyer as an initial response to a sneaky delay tactic. Foxes also have lawyers, and this will probably delay things even further. For all you know the owner's lawyer is a high school buddy willing to write a few letters for free while you're shelling out $175 per hour every time your attorney sneezes. Try to keep away from any legal action unless it's absolutely necessary. You should first use your own business acumen to confound sneaky delay tactics.

Don't Rely on Credit Checks

Credit checks are a good thing to do before consummating a sale with the fox but they're far from infallible. Just because a small business owner has a decent credit rating doesn't mean he's not above pulling a sneaky tactic or two on you now and again. Many small businesses don't even subscribe to the more common services like Dun & Bradstreet, and if they do they supply minimal information. Perform a credit check on a new customer for sure, but don't rely on the information entirely. You can investigate a prospective small customer's payment and legal history at many popular Web sites like *www.knowx.com.*

Break Down the Sale

A great way to make sure you don't lose too much money from a sneaky delay tactic or nonpayment is by breaking down your sale. Take a deposit and then get the remainder on success-ful delivery. Deliver one-third of what's promised and get paid for that amount. We had our kitchen redone a few months ago. Our contractor asked for a third at signing, a third when the cabinets were put in, and the balance on completion of the project. That way he wasn't as exposed to any sneaky delay tactics I might have chosen to employ. Do a little something first, get your money, then do a little more. Ship some of your product and get paid, then ship some more. Don't put all of your eggs in one basket if you can help it.

Strategies to Use Before the Invoice Comes Due

It's a fact that no matter how diligent you are and no matter how many precautions you may take in advance, once you've performed your service or shipped your product to the crazy fox you're now assuming the risk of collection and are exposed to sneaky delay tactics. But this doesn't mean you can't take some measures before the invoice is due to try and minimize the number of times you become a victim of a sneaky delay tactic. Here are a few things that may help.

Look at How the Big Boys Avoid Sneaky Delay Tactics

Many big businesses have figured out ways to avoid sneaky delay tactics from those wily foxes. Big businesses, of course, have more resources at their disposal to fight this war. They know the value of investing in good systems to handle collection. Wachovia Bank is a good example. Need a business loan from Wachovia? You'll probably be required to open a checking account with them so that scheduled payments can be automatically deducted each month.

Big companies are very good at delivering contracts and agreements that, in the worst-case scenario, provide strong legal basis for pursuing their claims. When we buy anything online from a nationally recognized office supply store we are required to provide a credit card, or cash on delivery, to ensure they do not fall victim to sneaky delay tactics. Many big companies take the time before a sale to assess their risks appropriately. There's a lot to learn from the big boys who sell to the little fish.

Make Pre-Emptive Strikes

If you suspect that a tricky little fox may be prone to a sneaky delay tactic or two, you might want to have someone from your office check in to see how things are going. Tactics such as the "good ol' country boy," "Houston, we have a problem," and "all systems shut down" can be marginalized if someone talks to the fox well before an invoice comes due. They can confirm whether or not he is satisfied and ask directly if there are any problems or issues. A crazy fox like Mitch may think it's great customer service but we know better. It's called protecting our investment.

Never Become Too Friendly

Be aware that your business relationship may be jeopardized if you decide to strike a friendship with your small business customer. For example, a good friend of mine asked if we would install one of our software products in his business and provide some training. Instead, I referred him to a friendly competitor and offered to act in a consulting capacity, free of charge. This way when I see my friend we can talk about baseball and politics, not his overdue invoices.

Allow Customers to Use Credit Cards

A few years ago we did a wonderful thing. We got a credit card machine. True, we're paying the monthly lease and the exorbitant fees. But the money we spent on collections decreased dramatically. Without a credit card machine we were forced to invoice and try to get our money at a future date. Or, in some cases, we would invoice and wait for payment before shipping product or performing a service.

Both of these tactics took extra administrative time and sometimes angered our customers. Now all we need to do is get a credit card number over the phone, pass it through the machine and bingo—it's approved and the money's in our account the next day. Dealing with foxes means that you're generally going to be dealing with more transactions for smaller dollar amounts. If this description somewhat fits your business then a great way to avoid many sneaky delay tactics is to start taking credit cards. I look at the extra fees as part of the cost operating in this environment, and adjust my pricing accordingly.

Deliver Everything You Promised

As we've seen with some of the sneaky delay tactics previously mentioned, a small oversight on your part may be pounced on by the ever-wily fox. Shipping one less item can easily cause an entire payment to be withheld. Performing all tasks but one can easily delay payment for a few more days. For those rascals that tend to pull one of these tactics, the best approach is to make doubly sure that you're delivering everything that you promised. And, after delivery, a quick phone call should be made by someone in your office to the customer to confirm receipt and that everything is working as it should. Make very certain that you did everything that you promised to do. This will help minimize (but not eliminate) the number of sneaky delay tactics that the crazy fox can try.

Foxy **TIP**

Get alerted before your invoices approaches thirty days old. Alerting software, like KnowledgeSync (www.vineyardsoft. com) *can help you avoid bad debts before they happen.*

Don't Count Your Chickens

The minute an invoice drops into the over-thirty-day column, brace yourself for a possible writeoff. You may have every intention of collecting 100 percent of the amount owed, but get ready for the fact that, in order to eke out a profit or at least maintain some dignity, you may be forced to lose something. If one of these foxes pulls a "Houston, we have a problem," then it is likely going to cost something extra for a service person to resolve any open issues, fabricated or not, in order to get the bill paid. If you're unlucky enough to encounter a "one for you, two for me" tactic, then realize that you are going to be faced with an arbitrary discount and will most likely have to write off some amount because it's not worth the additional cost to collect. In other words, don't count your chickens before they're hatched. Until the money is in the bank, you should regard every invoice as a potential collection issue.

Strategies for Being in Collection Mode

No matter how hard you try to avoid becoming a victim to a sneaky delay tactic it's going to happen. In the world of wily foxes, sneaky delay tactics are a fact of life. The game you can play is to minimize those sneaky delay tactics that actually turn into bad debt. According to a recent study, 7.5 percent of all businesses fail as a result of bad debt. This statistic demonstrates that a game of delay can easily turn into a not so funny situation of bad debt if it happens enough. Bad debts are a part of doing business in the small business environment but you must strive to make sure that one customer's delay won't have a catastrophic impact on your business. Once in the clutches of a sneaky delay tactic, respond vigorously. Here are some of the things you can do.

Use Disinterested Third Parties to Collect Your Money

Certain sneaky delay tactics are used to buy time and get extra services or products from the vendor. For example, a rascal who uses the "mousetrap" tactic effectively will manage to push off the payment of a vendor's invoice while at the same time enticing the vendor to visit his premises and squeeze a little extra work out of him. One way to sidestep this kind of tactic is by using a disinterested third party as the person who does the collection work. In our business, we send a third party who has no technical skills so they can't be roped into doing more work. We give them incentives for collecting overdue accounts so it's to their benefit to push past all sneaky delay tactics and get the money. If you've got such a person on staff, do your best to delegate collection activities to him or her so you can stay focused on the work at hand.

Respond with Aggressive and Loud Tactics

If a crazy fox decides to employ a sneaky delay tactic, he's now giving you justification to make some noise. Make it clear as soon as possible that you're wise to the tactic. Have someone from your office call him every day if necessary. Send reminder faxes and e-mails relentlessly. Make the fox feel sorry for even trying this tactic on you. Feel justified to annoy, irritate, aggravate and plain get on the nerves of your customer until he pays up . . . remember, he asked for it. If you're annoying enough, he may decide to try a sneaky delay tactic on someone else next time and pay your invoice within terms.

Foxy TIP

Getting paid from a small customer who went bankrupt is a real long shot. If you think bankruptcy is imminent for one of your clients then try and collect something before the paperwork is filed.

Take the Quickest Route and Lick Your Wounds

If you fall victim to a sneaky delay tactic then you can only be on the defensive. You have to look at any opportunity to get some of your money and take it. I didn't follow this advice once and really got burned. Jason, a customer of mine in financial trouble, offered me $3,000 cash on a $5,000 invoice due and asked if we could call it a day at that. I refused outright. The money would have covered my costs, but left me without a profit. Jason wound up closing up shop a few weeks later and instead of having my cost covered I lost it all.

I now know that when a late-paying little rogue like Jason is offering up something I take it and ask questions later, even if it's less than I hoped. On a few occasions I settled for fifty cents on the dollar to at least cover my costs and be done with the customer. Being stubborn is not always the best way to deal with a sneaky delay tactic.

Make a List, Check It Twice, and Never Be Too Nice

When you hear the familiar line of an "all systems shut down" tactic, like "Gee, I was about to pay your invoice, but we came across this little problem here . . . " you should gear up for battle. Just think about it: This rogue has *your* money and all you've got is a piece of paper that says he owes it to you. The only thing between you and your money is resolving some problem that he's made up to delay paying you.

Foxy **FACT**

The cost of borrowed funds is higher for small firms. Interest rates on bank loans for small businesses average 2 or 3 percentage points over the prime rate.

In my business, I reluctantly follow the same routine: I get on the phone with the wily little fox and agree on a "list" of open issues. I hand the list to a technician and instruct the technician to resolve each item on the list to both persons' satisfaction. Before sending the technician out, I receive a promise from the small business owner that there will be a check ready on site as long as the issues are satisfactorily resolved. They almost always are because there really were no significant issues to begin with, just a desire to buy a few more days of time.

Pay the Wily Fox an Off-Hours Visit to Catch Him in His Lair

Richard was a client of mine who owned an "everything for a dollar" store. He was famous for pulling sneaky delay tactics on us. Early on, before we figured him out, we were stuck holding his invoices for months. He loved to pull the "disappearing act" and "missing document" ploys. But we railroaded him. I got wise to his game. I would stop by (or have someone from my office stop by) Richard's store at unusual hours so as to get to him face to face. He was always a little easier to catch because he spent a lot of time in his store and it's a public place.

Not all foxes are so accessible. Tracking some of them down can be an investigative nightmare. For the more elusive rascals you may need to make it a point to appear at off-times. Stopping by during off-hours also reduces your risk of the "mousetrap" tactic as well—it may be too early or late to actually perform any services. Many of these foxes like to work Saturday mornings. Still others can be found very, very early in the day or very late in the evening. Without their gatekeepers around, you may find your customer picking up the phone at eight in the morning or very late at night. Then you can attack!

Discount What's Said, Especially Claims of Poverty

A crazy fox may claim a shortage of cash, but didn't you notice a new Lexus parked outside? And wasn't he calling you from his beach house at the time? Among certain foxes, "poor" is definitely a relative term. It may have nothing to do with actual circumstances. Rather, it's connected to the emotional state of the business owner at the time. Here are two things you should know:

1. Most of the time, the fox has the money, no matter what you're being told.
2. He is probably choosing to spend money elsewhere rather than paying what he owes you.

There may be other vendors that take priority over you. For example, I know that Richard's wholesaler will get his money before I will get mine. I also know that Ken, a construction client of mine, will pay his subcontractors and employees first before he considers my computer service fees. Make your response firm and consistent. Ask the fox point-blank when he's going to have the money and follow up tenaciously until you are paid.

Strategies for the Follow-Up Sale

Amazingly, no matter how devious, sneaky, cunning, and crafty some foxes prove to be, people are still willing to do business with many of them again. I have continued to sell product to complete scoundrels. I provide services to known rascals. I do work for villains who have played every sneaky delay tactic in the book with me. Why? Because I've learned which of my foxes I can make a profit on and which ones I can't. I've also learned which foxes are not worth the bother no matter how much profit is involved.

Let Your Customers Decide

Try to be prepared to handle those 20 percent of your small business customers who create 80 percent of your problems. If a fox has tried a sneaky delay tactic or two on you in the past, try not to walk away unless you see no way to make a profit from him. For example, I fell victim to numerous sneaky delay tactics played on me by of one of my slimier former clients, Malcolm, head of Keller Associates. I once gave him the benefit of the doubt after he played the "Houston, we have a problem" tactic following a service call. On our next visit, I became frustrated when Malcolm tried the "all systems shut-down approach."

I ultimately lost my patience after falling victim to the "good 'ol country boy" routine when he explained that his nonpayment was due to a lack of training and understanding of the new software we sold him. For our next job I firmly quoted him rates that were 50 percent higher. He sputtered and barked and eventually we parted ways, but at least the choice was his and it was he who ultimately decided to part ways. Let your foxes decide if they want to walk from you. Price them accordingly. You may earn more profits by losing this customer than by keeping him around. But if he stays, you get your bonus.

Have a Long Memory

Before agreeing to the next deal, try saying reminding them of their past behavior. For example, you could say something like, "Now, if there is a problem, you're going to tell me sooner this time, right?" You can be crazy just like him. Everyone's allowed to make a mistake, but if you fall victim to the same sneaky delay tactic played on you by the same customer then you get what you deserve! Try being tongue in cheek, but at the same time, make it clear that you're serious with your message. The customer will be less likely to try a delay tactic if they know they are going to get busted.

Match Payment with Performance

Rodney, is a manufacturer of made-to-order industrial vacuums. When busy, Rodney employs about fifty to sixty people. He deals with a lot of wily foxes. Over the eight years I've known

Rodney, he has managed to impress me as one of the best cash flow managers I've ever seen. He rarely falls for sneaky delay tactics. His contracts match deliverables with payments and provide for work stoppage if violated. He often receives a deposit up front and has a job costing system so detailed that he can tell weeks in advance when his costs will match cash received and avoid being in a collection situation.

Break down your agreement into smaller pieces and get paid for each milestone. If you receive an order for 1,000 units, ship 500, get paid, and then ship the rest. If you're selling insurance to the fox, get an initial deposit before initiating the policy and then match the policy period to the payment. If you're providing a professional service then be sure to charge a "setup fee" and then match and get paid for each service before providing the next. For most small customers, this practice will eventually become unnecessary. But for those few wily ones, it can save you big-time.

Foxy **TIP**

Review your files a few times a year and remove those unprofitable, nonpaying rogues from your contact list. The ocean is filled with better fish to fry.

Think Long Term

Your response to a sneaky delay tactic is going to depend on what you'd like your long-term relationship to be with this fox. For some customers, you'll accept a certain amount of grief. But for others you may decide that the long-term benefits just aren't worth it. Bob Smith, from Sandy Run Corporation, was one cad who, from the moment we began putting together our project, nickel-and-dimed us throughout the entire process. That, plus his annoying personality, rubbed me the wrong way and made me regret ever agreeing to the job. We got the "upfront disclaimer" throughout the sales process and, sure enough, his invoice came due and no payment was received. I knew from that moment that there was no long-term future with this rascal. I could see that the future revenue opportunities from Sandy Run Corporation would be significantly outweighed by both hard and soft costs.

Bake It in Later

If you have clients with whom you know a long-term future is still possible, take extra steps to make sure everything is done to their satisfaction so you can get paid. Record any extra hours that you spend over and above what is fair in the customer's record, and the next time they propose a project or need you to perform additional services, find ways to "bake-in" that time elsewhere. Is this underhanded? Are you deceptively padding your invoice with extra fees? Do you feel a little uncomfortable doing this? Welcome to the world of small business. Take a look at what your suppliers are doing to you right now. What exactly is "shipping and handling" anyway? How come your bank is charging you that one-time "administration fee" for setting up a checking account? Why are some prices slightly higher for no apparent reason? Is undercoating for that new car really necessary? Big companies hide extra fees and charges everywhere—whatever you call it, it's more revenue to them.

Strategies That *Don't* Work with the Wily Fox

I'm sorry to say that I've had the misfortune of having to employ all of the above strategies. They do work. In the business environment it's important to have a good offense. You must be prepared for the inevitable sneaky delay tactic before it happens. However, there are certain strategies that, while commonly used, are just not effective in collecting money from a small business customer. Here are a few counter-tactics that could only be used to collect money from a large customer, not a small one.

Taking It to the Top

If someone at a larger client is being a pain the neck, you always have the option of bumping the problem upstairs. By going to the boss, you may find someone with a more sympathetic ear. You may be able to garner some empathy or state your case differently. An employee at a larger company is often concerned with what the boss thinks. If you prove that the employee acted unprofessionally or irrationally you may not only get paid but also embarrass the employee. This tactic wouldn't work with a small business owner. Wily foxes could not care less. Their only boss is the customer. They can be as crazy as they want to be. You can't go over their head. The buck stops with them.

Foxy TIP

Some small customers are preparing to be large one day. These types of business owners are more sensitive to bad press. Keep this weapon in mind.

The Threat of Bad Publicity

When I was working at my former employer, a large client of mine received an unsolicited letter in the mail from a sole attorney who threatened a class action lawsuit. The suit alleged misleading remarks made by the company's CEO at an industry conference. After much deliberation, the company sent this attorney a $100,000 check to settle with him and avoid the lawsuit and its potential embarrassment.

One letter turned into a six-figure payout. What a great idea, huh? Simply because the company didn't want the bad press. Larger companies are much more concerned about their image than the small business owner. They have public relations firms, marketing departments, and advertising agencies. They make charitable donations and contribute to the community. They don't like bad press. They're sensitive to disputes that would cast them in a poor light. If the issue is important enough, an unhappy creditor can always take the company to court, spread the information, place unflattering advertisements and the like. The typical large company would need to respond in some way so as to avoid any bad PR. You can't play this game with a wily fox.

Compartmentalizing Problems

As a manager at my former employer, another of my clients was a large chemical company. They had subsidiaries all over the world. I managed projects at many of these locations. Because the company was decentralized we billed each facility as the work was done. It was not uncommon to have collection and billing issues with one subsidiary while we continued work at another. The company was so big that it was business as usual with one part of the organization while at the same time we were in a heated dispute with another subsidiary about an open bill.

Even though this was one client, we had to compartmentalize problems. We didn't let the failure to pay from one division of the company affect the work we were doing with another. This would never fly at a small business. One invoice affects the entire relationship. A good small business owner knows what's going on at all of his locations. There is no compartmentalization.

Summary

Mitch continues to be a great client of ours. Just last month we helped him with another project. And this time I paid close attention. We kept our rates per hour at standard and gave no breaks. We broke the project out into four pieces and made sure payment was received before moving on to the next phase. Every conversation was confirmed by e-mail to Mitch and his computer guy so there was no convenient lapse of memory. We gave conservative (translation: higher than normal) estimates of time spent to cover ourselves. In short, I gave Mitch no benefit of the doubt. Through all of our conversations about our vacations, our kids' sports activities and our mutual business ownership problems I never forgot Mitch's earlier brazen methods for not paying me. I had learned such a painful lesson that time that I vowed not to make the same mistake with him again. And I didn't. When collecting money from the fox, it helps to have a memory like an elephant.

Beyond Lip Service

Shape Up Your Organization to Keep a Demanding Fox Happy

Kristin is a tough fox to service. Kristin runs a profitable small trucking company called KRJ Transport. She took over the business from her dad just out of high school and after driving a truck herself for five years. She's tough because her job is tough. She has to make sure that fifty independent, and often unreliable, drivers pick up and deliver product on time. As you can imagine, she's under a great deal of stress. Missing drivers, mechanical breakdowns, insurance claims, speeding tickets, rotting produce, road detours, and complaining customers are a normal part of her chaotic day. But Kristin runs a tight ship. She takes no bull. She curses, yells, and throws insults as well as any of her drivers. She does business with all sorts of interesting characters.

Kristin is quite a character herself. Diplomatic is not exactly how I'd describe her. Coarse, rough, and abrasive are words that more readily come to mind. Impatient, demanding, and intense are others. But she knows how to make a buck. And she also knows how to save a few pennies, too.

Servicing a fox like Kristin is not easy. For example, one day the accounting system we sold her went down. This was not an insignificant problem. Kristin's accounting database is the heart of her business. She books orders and does all of her billing in the system. She tracks costs, processes payroll, and keeps most of her customer information there. She stores billing, delivery, personal, and regulatory info for each customer and driver in this system as well. So when it went down you can imagine her reaction. We received a frantic call from her at about nine in the morning and continued to receive frantic calls from her at fifteen-minute intervals until one of our service people showed up at her place. She wouldn't relent until she had someone there to fix her problem.

Foxy **FACT**

Forty percent of small businesses are owned by women.

Our technician repaired her database and had her back up and running within a couple of hours. The problem was that Kristin really drove him nuts. For example, he needed to order special software to fix some of her workstations. She warily peppered him with questions about why this was necessary. Reluctantly she authorized the purchase right then and there. But she continued to watch over his shoulder as he did his work. This was really distracting. She kept track of every minute he spent. She complained when she thought he was taking too long to do something. She second-guessed some of his work. She was disappointed that he had to call the software manufacturer's support department on one issue instead of knowing the answer himself. And she got irritated when things started taking longer than she anticipated.

My technician was happy to get out of there. Not surprisingly, and though we were there within hours and fixed her very critical computer system, she still protested about the cost of the visit. Plus, she took more than sixty days to pay our bill. Now brace yourself: Kristin is what I'd call a good small customer!

It's not an easy job to profitably service a crazy fox like Kristin. She's busy doing so many other things that she often has to rely on outsiders for help. And she doesn't like this. She's afraid of being ripped off. She doesn't like people digging into her business affairs unless it's absolutely necessary. She's sensitive to being treated like the little fish that she is. She's constantly trying to figure out what it takes to keep things working for the least amount of money possible. She demands dependability and fast action. But she absolutely loves a bargain, even if it's at the expense of the best service possible. She cares a whole lot more about what's being done then any person working for a larger company ever will. She's loyal to those suppliers that deliver something to her fast, good enough, and cheap. She'll do whatever it takes to fix a problem, even if it means cutting a corner here or there. We've got lots of small clients like Kristin who all need a different service approach as compared to our larger customers. There are definitely unique challenges when providing service to the clever and (and sometimes) crazy fox.

The Unique Challenges of Serving the Fox

Many people think that getting a small business owner to buy their product is the toughest part of the process. However, those who provide ongoing service to these foxes know that the toughest challenges lie after the sale. When a small business owner signs a service contract, don't expect to sit back, relax, and let the checks roll in. Your dreams of a long and profitable relationship may be far-fetched if your company is not prepared to provide the kind of satisfactory, yet affordable, service that a typical fox requires. This type of service presents a vendor with different challenges than doing the same for a larger company. It's not easy to do it right, and still make money, because of the numbers involved. It may take ten small business service contracts to equal the dollar value of one service contract with a larger company. The cost structure to service this type of model is not the same. It takes a different organizational structure to profitably service small business owners.

More on Their Minds

To illustrate, consider James. He is a client of mine and a clever fox who owns and operates a very successful neighborhood pizza shop. A father of three who spends twelve hours a day making pizzas and barking orders, James is a great example of why a fox needs a lot of special attention to service, as compared to their corporate counterpart.

For starters, small business owners like James have to worry about more things than someone from a larger company. I have a friend who's a purchasing manager at a division of a large insurance company in the Midwest. He called me once because his department was looking for a software application that could help him manage purchase orders. We spent a great deal of time together evaluating the purchase order module of one of the accounting applications we sell. During this exercise I thought just how different this process was as compared to the small business clients I normally deal with.

If I were undertaking the same exercise with someone like James, we would not only be looking at the purchase order module, but also the modules for point-of-sale transactions, inventory, payables, payroll, and general ledger. My college-educated friend at the insurance company is a smart person, yet he had the benefit of applying his smarts to one specific challenge—evaluating a single module of an accounting system that affected his job. Our intrepid fox, James, armed with only a high school diploma, needed to evaluate an entire accounting system, with a much greater impact on his entire business.

Throughout the day, a busy fox like James meets with his banker, searches to replace employees who don't show up for work, negotiates with the bakery, argues with a delivery driver, and fights with repairmen. Contrast that with my friend in the insurance company whose primary responsibility is negotiating pricing with his vendors. James has a lot on his mind and he needs help from an organization that is structured to understand his entire business, not just a little part of it. Is your staff trained to look at their fox's entire business and provide the kind of advice a business owner really needs?

Diplomacy Is Rare

In general, foxes tend to be less diplomatic in their dealings with others compared to their larger company counterparts. They are overworked, stressed, short of resources and as result may be less sensitive to someone's feelings and professional courtesies. However, don't assume that just because your small business customer doesn't act "professionally" he's not a good businessperson.

There are many ways to express one's dissatisfaction with a product or service. An employee from a larger company, wishing to appear professional and under pressure to not represent their company in a negative may politely say that your product isn't meeting their expectations and wish you good luck in the future. Our friend James, on the other hand, will probably express his view directly, such as "this product *stinks!*"

When providing service to a crazy fox like James, be prepared for the unedited truth. Remember that because James is the boss. There are few people that will tell him when he's behaving coarsely. Even a CEO at a large company has to answer to a board of directors and shareholders. Anyone who's seen James in action would agree that he would barely last a day in a big company environment. He's got a quick tongue and pulls no punches. This fox is going to say what's on his mind because that's the way he is. Try not to let it shock you. Is your staff specially taught how to service dozens of sometimes grumpy, undiplomatic foxes every day?

The Education Issue

Another reason why it's so different serving a small business is the educational background of the people employed by your customer. Small firms are more likely than large businesses to hire employees on the margin of the labor force. Although lacking in education, many of these employees are good workers who can be hired at a much lower cost. Small businesses don't do their recruiting on college campuses like many larger companies. Most of James's employees are high school kids—in fact, James barely finished high school himself.

Also, one out of five employees at small companies are part-time. This is a much higher percentage than what you'll find at larger companies. Fifty-four percent of small business employees only have a high school degree or less, compared with 44 percent in large firms. When servicing small companies you must be prepared to work with people who come from very diverse backgrounds and may lack formal education. For this reason, employees at small businesses may need extra time to understand how to do something and may not be used to researching questions on their own. Anticipate more service time when working with small businesses.

Foxy TIP

Small business owners expect an unreasonably quick response. Acknowledge their problems immediately.

Impatience Is the Watchword

Foxes can be more impatient than their counterparts at larger organizations, where most employees are somewhat used to waiting for certain things to happen. Small business owners can't imagine waiting for anything important for very long. But at a larger company, it is standard practice. Employees at larger companies are accustomed to waiting for things, because they're used to myriad internal procedures and bureaucracy involved to get anything done. Small business owners rule their businesses and generally get their own way. Foxes are impatient and don't like to wait for others. Is your organization prepared to respond fast to your fox's impatient demands?

Lack of Self-Confidence

Foxes may initially need a lot more attention from your service staff than a larger company. This may be due to apprehension. I'm working with one prospective customer right now, a small metals manufacturer, who has agonized for more than two years about purchasing a new computer system for managing his sales and administrative staff. Each time I talk to him, he wavers. He always has questions and he's never convinced. The entire system would run him about $10,000 complete with training. Two weeks ago, I found out that he purchased a new cutting machine for $150,000. One of his employees told me he made the decision after one visit from the manufacturer—it was a no-brainer. He knew what he was buying. My prospective customer knows his knowledge is lacking, and he is wary of a vendor taking advantage of him.

A small business customer like James may know how to make a great pizza but he doesn't know the first thing about phone systems or computers. He's rarely had the opportunity to supervise others, with maybe the exception of his children. Unlike a counterpart at a larger company, he can't turn to another internal resource for help and rarely has the inclination to solicit outside assistance.

Larger companies have finance departments that are trained to look at financial contracts, production foremen who are experienced at buying equipment, sales managers who are practiced with different types of commission plans, and marketing staff who can question advertising rates and proposals. Our hero doesn't have these kinds of resources and therefore must rely more on a vendor's advice. So when a problem does occur he may find himself more defensive about the situation and less inclined to reasonably discuss a solution. He's aware of the exposure caused by his own ignorance.

You should prepare yourself to spend the extra time explaining how you've fixed a problem, and you shouldn't think badly of a cautious fox like James if he's suspicious at first. Eventually, he'll learn to trust that you are not taking advantage of him, and he'll be more open to the fact that he's not as knowledgeable about your expertise as he might think.

Are you patient enough to build this kind of relationship? Is your organization constructed to handle this long-term approach?

Flexible Like a Rubber Band

On a more positive note, many foxes can be a lot more flexible than someone who works at a larger company. Remember when our technician needed to order special software to fix some of Kristin's workstations? The same situation at a larger company would probably require the involvement of the IT staff and who knows who else from purchasing and accounting. However, Kristin could (albeit reluctantly) approve the acquisition quickly and actually helped with the download herself while my guy worked on another matter. If an important piece of equipment breaks, I know that James would do whatever it takes to get it fixed, like paying a little extra to the repairman who's coming after hours.

Foxes don't have to wait for management approval to authorize a quick spend on something important. They all can, at the spur of a moment, decide to defer payment to a nonperforming vendor in lieu of someone who needs the money sooner. If you come up with a solution to a problem that's even a little unique, the typical fox won't have to worry that his job is on the line if he takes a chance. Many foxes like James will be more likely to accept a workaround solution to a problem that impacts their business than an employee at a larger company. Are your service people trained to think on their feet and potentially cut a few corners or break a couple of rules to get the job done?

The Four Laws to Successfully Service the Crazy Fox

Now that we've recognized that servicing these demanding foxes requires a different organizational approach than servicing larger customers, we can turn to some ways for doing it right. Whenever you have a particular service issue with a small customer you should look to these four laws to keep yourself focused. Even when you satisfy all of them, your customer may still be unhappy. It's a simple fact in business that you can't please everyone all of the time. Fortunately, there are a lot more foxes in the woods.

Law #1: Always Say Please and Thank You

Kristin feels like she's the little fish in the pond. She has to shout loud just to get heard. She feels that she doesn't garner the same kind of respect that a larger customer earns. She knows that her spending levels will never compete with the big boys. Her days are filled arguing with suppliers, chasing down drivers, and trying to collect money from other foxes who are playing sneaky delay tactics with her.

So be polite and upbeat. The fox needs a little compassion. Respect and consideration will go a long way. Your service department should stress politeness and being nice as its top priority. A typical fox, even a tough one like Kristin, needs more tender loving care than the larger customer. She wants to be treated like the big customer that she's not. Your service relationship will be extremely strong if you make sure your service people always say please and thank you. In other words, be respectful, positive, friendly and fun. That goes a long way with the small business customer.

Law #2: Always Do What You Say You're Going to Do

Foxes are used to people breaking their commitments. Employees call in sick. Scheduled service calls get bumped for emergencies at other, higher-paying customers. Promises are often made that aren't kept. Foxes themselves are not innocent in this game. A small business owner will often commit to a service or job to get desperately needed revenue or new customer and later question how the heck they're going to get it done with the limited resources they know they have. So imagine the fox's surprise when you always do what you say you're going to do.

If you promise same-day service, deliver it. If you promise to call back within an hour, call back—even if you are still working on the problem. If you say you're completely booked but will be there on Monday, then be sure to get there on Monday, even if it requires overtime for your staff or a long day for you. Because there's less money at stake, the fox finds himself the victim of delays, deferrals, and deceit more often than the large customer. Always do what you say you're going to do and your foxes will love you. In today's world, this reliability is not as common as you may think.

Law #3: Always Show Up on Time

Like a lot of other foxes, Kristin is a very busy person. She starts her day very early and ends it long after a lot of corporate managers have clocked out. She doesn't have scheduled coffee breaks or personal time. She's always running around, putting out fires, trying to keep the ship pointed in the right direction. When we have to visit her offices to fix even one computer, we know that our visit is going to significantly disrupt her business. We look at it this way: If one workstation out of five in her company is undergoing service by us, that means that 20 percent of her workforce is incapacitated until the work is finished.

When servicing your small business customer always show up on time. A wasted hour or two is absorbed into the big company's corporate overhead structure. That same amount of time is a critical expense to the busy fox who can't afford to put up with lateness or unreliability for very long.

Law #4: Always Finish What You Start

Let's face the unspoken fact: Foxes tend to get less respect than larger companies. Service jobs are always less in scope and companies that have to provide service to smaller customers often sandwich those jobs between the jobs they're doing for the big boys. Frequently, workers or technicians are pulled off the small jobs and sent to the bigger ones when the need exists. This is not a good way to do business in the small business marketplace. Not finishing what you start is an easy way to lose a lot of good customers.

Important Tools You'll Need to Service the Fox

If you're going to be doing business in the small business marketplace, you'll probably need some of the following tools for the unique service requirements you'll encounter.

Foxy TIP

An answering service is no substitute for a service desk. Make every effort to have your qualified people answer the phone.

A Thick Skin

Bite your lower lip, steel your eyes, and leave your feelings at home. Even on a good day, some foxes can be rude, obnoxious, demanding, impatient, and downright unfriendly. Employees at big companies need to maintain some semblance of corporate professionalism. Foxes just need to get it done, and personal feelings are not a priority. As strong as our relationship has been, Kristin has, on numerous occasions, screamed at our technicians, harassed us with phone calls, and complained unabashedly about our shortcomings. And that's when she's in a good mood. Of course, two days later and after her problem's been fixed, she's back to being cordial. Wear your thickest skin when servicing those few wacky foxes. Insults, curse words, inflammatory comments and verbal abuse have to bounce off your hardened exterior and not compromise your performance.

A Dedicated Service Desk

If you're going to provide services to a fox you'll need someone in your company dedicated to fielding and responding to service calls. I've made the mistake over the years of having our onsite technicians also field telephone calls while out in the field. Frequently, this practice annoyed the client who was being visited as well as the client on the phone. The small business owner isn't used to waiting for answers from their employees, and they are certainly not going to put up with waiting for service from you if they can help it. They don't want to talk to an answering machine, or to a tech in the field dividing his time between clients. The fox wants to talk to someone who's dedicated to the service effort and who can give them the full attention that they feel they deserve.

In the small business marketplace, you'll need to do business with a lot of these foxes at the same time, not just a handful of big customers. What if they all start calling at once? What if 10 percent of these customers suddenly have a problem on any given day? A dedicated service desk is critical for handling the load. Make sure you've got the right staffing in place.

Round-the-Clock Response

The typical fox does not clock in at nine and clock out at five. He is always working. One of the best things about running your own company is that you do have more flexibility with your time. Kristin arrives at work every day before 6:30 A.M. while her husband gets their kids off to school. She leaves at 3:00 P.M. to collect her kids but by 7:00 P.M. she's doing the day's unfinished paperwork at home. Many times she returns to the office in the evenings. Her schedule is anything but consistent. Most managers at large companies, while putting in the occasional overtime, work off a schedule that is often highly correlated to their boss's routine. When I was a controller at a pharmaceutical company, I remember marking my arrival and departure times ten minutes before and after the chief financial officer.

If you want to make your small business customers happy, your service operation has to be working and available 24/7. Like a doctor's office, someone should always be on call. The small business owner should feel as comfortable reaching a technician at eleven in the evening as she would at two in the afternoon.

A Current Accounts Receivable Ledger

If you pay then I'll play! A current listing of your open accounts receivable is a crucial tool for doing service in the small business marketplace. As we've discussed earlier, some of your foxes may be a little villainous. These specific rascals may try lots of tricks to get product or services from you without paying (or at least to delay payment). Your biggest leverage is their need for continuing service. Don't get hoodwinked. Service shouldn't be performed for these few scalawags who have overdue invoices. It's not fair to be asked to perform more work when you haven't been paid for the work you've already done.

Whenever a fox calls, your service desk should have immediate access to that customer's accounts receivable ledger. This can be on a daily printed report or through your company's accounting system. For overdue accounts asking for more service, your technicians should turn the sly little fox over to accounting immediately and not get involved in any collection discussions (we'll discuss this more later). Serve your paying customers. Defer those who have deferred you.

Reliable Service Desk Software

There are great help desk applications available today, ranging in price from a few hundred dollars to several thousand. Our service desk application automatically sends e-mails and alerts to our technicians the minute a service call request is received from a fox. It allows the technician in the field to update and close tickets on a handheld computer or online. It can allow our foxes to login to our Web site, open new tickets, or check on the status of an existing ticket. Many of these applications have built in automation to open tickets and if, for example, a ticket is open more than two hours, escalate it to someone else. The software can notify your service department in advance of any pending warranty or contract expirations.

Because of the market you've chosen, your profitability will rely on handling a larger volume of problems efficiently. If you're serious about performing great service to a lot of foxes, and making money at it, it's critical that you invest in good service desk technology.

A Good Communications System

A good communications system is imperative to successfully service small business customers. If Kristin doesn't hear from someone within ten minutes of making a call for service, she's going to start calling back demanding attention.

Like many businesses, our company uses cell phones and pagers. Some companies use long-range walkie-talkies. Our technicians frequently check their e-mail and service calls online. Others successfully employ wireless handhelds to receive information. Busy and impatient foxes need attention yesterday. They're calling about a problem that was probably a problem two weeks ago but only got bad enough to disrupt them today. So now it's your problem. All of these devices are extremely important to your service desk.

Foxy TIP

Walkie-talkie phone services are the quickest way to communicate. Many of your small business customers already use them.

Latitude

One very important tool you'll need can't be purchased. It's *latitude*. Latitude is a state of mind. Remember that nothing will go as planned. Because you're working in the crazy world of foxes, you'll be dealing with people who are pretty disorganized. You're going to have to put out fires every day. Their problems will quickly become your problems. Having latitude means giving oneself room to maneuver. It means leaving enough breathing space to handle the inevitable disasters that will happen every single day. In the small business environment, you're working on very thin margins that depend on getting as much service done as possible.

Volume is key to making a profit in the small business market. However, if you don't give yourself enough latitude you're going to shoot yourself in the foot. If you schedule service visits back to back, leaving no room for potential problems, you're going to get in a bind. If you're basing your assignments on the slim hope that everything's going to go okay, you're fooling yourself. Expect that the worst will happen. Because it will. These are sometimes crazy foxes you're dealing with. Schedule your people accordingly. Leave blank spaces in their day. Don't worry; something will come up. Don't put yourself in a position where you're promising something to your small business customers and then breaking those promises because something else happened that turned your schedule upside down.

A General Knowledge Base for Quick Answers

KRJ Transportation does not have a research department. They don't do development. They don't have a company library or extensive databases of information. Kristin doesn't keep notes. And you know what annoys her the most? When she calls us with a problem that happened to her before, which we fixed, and we can't give her a quick answer back about how to fix it again. "You already fixed it once," she'll bark at our technician. "Can't you remember what you did?" Or how about: "I can't believe I'm the only one of your clients that has this problem!" Well, she's right. Foxes don't like to wait around. They need an answer, any answer, right now.

It's no excuse that our technician is on vacation, out to lunch, or with another client. Can't somebody else help? Every minute spent researching and solving a problem is costing both you and your fox money. And you can't afford these additional costs considering how little you're making off the fox to begin with. Create a knowledge base and disseminate the information widely. (A knowledge base can be kept in Microsoft Access, which you probably already own but might not know you have!)

Make the effort to have manuals. Buy database software and construct a place where information can be centrally stored. Make this database available on the Web for your customers and remote technicians. Be careful to implement procedures to make sure that the knowledge getting into such a system is accurate and stays up to date. Update your foxes frequently with newsletters. Create user-friendly help documents and how-to videos for both technicians and customers to use. Get them the answers as fast as possible. Your razor-thin margins depend on it.

The Right People

Foxes hate it when a good service person is no longer available. Remember that small businesses tend to be relationship businesses. Their employees may be family members, thus foxes are used to having a comfort level with people they work with. So compensate your best people more than the average. Give them extra perks. Offer them performance-based bonuses, stock options, or profit-sharing benefits. If an employee is happy, don't rock the boat. More importantly, if your small business customer is happy with a certain employee, don't change the recipe. At one of my former jobs, the best people would be pulled off their assignments and sent to larger accounts. This used to infuriate my smaller clients.

Take extra steps to keep your best employees. Promote further education. All great companies who successfully service the small business market strongly encourage their technicians to stay certified in their chosen field. Dealing with foxes takes unique skills—technical as well as psychological. Have your people get certified in what they do (if such a certification exists). Push them into getting skills needed for better customer service. Subscribe to industry trades and send them to industry conferences. Don't be afraid to make your employees more knowledgeable than you are.

Summary

I would love to say that having an unparalleled service operation for your foxes is what it's all about. But it's not. It's all about the money. Foxes don't really care about you or your business. They care about their business, their bank account, and surviving the month! They are not impressed by state-of-the-art computer systems, glossy documents, or fancy-looking invoices. They need you to solve a problem and then not bother them.

All of the tools and techniques discussed in this chapter are not for the benefit of your foxes. They're for your benefit. Your primary goal should be performing the best service possible and profitable for your company. If a certain fox is not profitable to your company, no matter whose fault it is, it is your responsibility to change your relationship with them. Your profitable foxes want you to stay in business.

Compared to many larger organizations, a crazy fox like James could be a loyal customer to the service provider who does a good job for him. A larger restaurant can have multiple vendors for a product and can afford to maintain expenditures with these vendors to keep in their favor. The fox may play some tricks to extend his invoice to you, but he doesn't want to go too far if he has a good relationship with you and knows you or your company is reliable. Most foxes are usually committed and loyal customers. So long as the job is done well, they won't spend the little time they have to search for alternative sources and will more likely than not stick with what works. But be wary. One advantage a clever fox has over a larger company is the ability to make changes faster. This change could be replacing you with someone else if you don't service them correctly.

Is the Customer Really Always Right?

Exploding Ten Small Business Customer Service Myths

Ted used to be a client of mine. But no more. I made the mistake of thinking that the tried-and-true customer service rules applied to a fox like Ted. Unfortunately, I got burned.

Six months after purchasing an accounting software application from us, I got a call from Ted, the owner of Waterside Corporation, a distributor of containers for the food industry. He was livid. "I want my money back or you'll hear from my attorneys!" he screamed at me over the phone. I was surprised. The last time I talked to Ted was six weeks earlier. That conversation went great. All seemed fine.

We had done our best to provide a high level of customer service to Ted during his implementation. We followed the rules. We did everything he had asked us to do, even when we didn't necessarily agree. We treated him with a high amount of professional courtesy, even when he didn't reciprocate. We gave him the exact same amount of attention that we gave all of our clients, even though it was obvious he needed a lot more. After we finished our training we left him alone to his devices so he could keep his costs down, as he requested. We tried not to raise his expectations too high and we felt we delivered more service than he bargained for.

But all was not well. He had made no progress since we last spoke. "In fact, I've gone backward. Your program doesn't calculate gross profit correctly. It doesn't let us enter in our orders the way we want. It runs too slowly and is giving me error messages. It's not user-friendly. We hate it. We want a refund!"

I knew the facts weren't important to Ted in his current state of mind. This fox could care less about the contract he signed over six months before in which stipulated no refunds or returns. Ted just wanted his money back. How could this be? We thought we had done everything right.

I tried to go the extra mile. I offered to immediately provide Ted with five days of service at almost half our rate to see if we couldn't get him out of his jam. But Ted didn't want to pay any more, period. I thought that delivering results, even at an extra cost, would satisfy Ted. But he was only going to be satisfied if it didn't cost him anything. Unfortunately, we parted ways on the most unfriendly of terms.

Alas, the standard rules of customer service rules didn't work in this case. We had done everything a good customer service group should do. But Ted was still very unhappy with us. The fox operates by his own set of customer service rules.

The Ten Service Myths—and Why They're Myths

Many standard customer service rules are nothing more than myths in the small business world. Foxes just can't be serviced like everyone else. Let's take a look at some of the more famous customer service recommendations and see why they're a falsehood in the small business environment.

Myth #1: "The customer's always right."

A fox is clever and sometimes crazy. But he's certainly not always right. And a true partner will tell him so. Managers who buy products and services at a large company are responsible for their areas at the company. The human resources manager may be looking to replace a company benefit plan. The product manager may be looking for a new piece of equipment. The vice president of marketing may be purchasing a special list of prospects. The controller is looking for new office furniture. Their needs are more specific. They consult with many others at their company. They often have a purchasing department who's job it is to negotiate and execute the buy. And depending on the size of the purchase there's normally several individuals involved in the chain of approval who will all contribute their opinions and knowledge in some way.

Ted's not a computer guy, or an accountant, or a warehouse specialist. Yet there he was, charged with implementing an accounting system that impacted every area of his business. I had assumed he knew what he was doing, but how could he know it all? I found out the customer's not always right, especially a small business customer.

I believed Ted when he told me he needed a system to help him manage inventory. But he was wrong. He really desired a system to track purchase orders for inventory that was coming in to his warehouse from overseas. He told me he needed a "typical" system for tracking freight. Incorrect! What he actually needed was something to track three types of freight and duty taxes imposed on his overseas business. He told me nothing was unusual in his payroll. Really? In fact, he had established a very unique employee loan program that was different for each employee. All of these issues had a major impact on the type of computer system that would have been right for him. We knew this and said nothing.

I didn't ask the questions when I should have. I went with the typical myth that the customer's always right. I should have realized that a fox like Ted wouldn't have the time to know the details of his purchase order, order entry, and freight process all at the same time. A typical fox like Ted has to be an expert at many more things than his counterpart at a larger company. Just because he's clever, resourceful and intelligent, don't ever believe that the fox is always right. He's not. And the really smart foxes know they're not always right, no matter what you're seeing on the outside. Challenge them.

Myth #2: "Customers care about results, not cost."

Baloney. Ted, and most resourceful small business owners like Ted, care a great deal about cost.

Even though I offered a substantial discount to get him out of a bind, he still wasn't biting. It wasn't only the result he wanted. He wanted it for free! A fox is used to getting things done quickly and will often tell the service team do "whatever it takes" to take care of a problem. Unfortunately, this posture changes radically once the service has been performed. Suddenly the fox that would "pay anything to get it done" finds himself questioning your "outrageous" invoice. When providing a service to the fox, remember that cost really is everything. Many small customers will live with all sorts of problems in because they just don't want to pay to fix it. If it's good enough, then it's good enough.

Foxy **TIP**

When cost is the primary concern, break your product delivery or services into phases to smooth out the cash flow impact.

Many foxes still use antiquated and inadequate systems to run their businesses. Larger corporations have the budgets to keep things up to date and in good working order if they need to. A bigger company can strive for perfection. The thrifty fox wants what's best for the price he's willing to pay. He'll settle for mediocrity if the job gets done satisfactorily. Ted was not getting his results from his system. If I had offered to help him for free he would have jumped at the opportunity. But this was not the case. He was willing to throw the whole thing out the door rather than pay an extra few dollars to make things right.

Never believe the "whatever it takes" command. For your typical fox you should be thinking that it's whatever he can afford. Match the delivery with his budget. Make sure that, for the money, the end result will be good enough in the fox's eyes.

Myth #3: "Always treat your customer with politeness and professionalism."

Not in the small business market! Treat the fox like he deserves to be treated—honestly and without pretense. Serving or selling your product to a large corporation requires a certain professional etiquette. Voices are rarely raised. Advice is delivered in a very diplomatic manner. Everyone tries to treat each other politely. There's always a risk that one of the multiple people involved in a conventional corporate relationship may feel insulted or slighted. Care is taken to treat everyone with a high level of respect and courtesy.

Foxy **FACT**

A survey showed that 92 percent of small business owners were aware they could file their taxes electronically, but only 58 percent did so.

Unfortunately, this type of behavior often doesn't apply in the small business world.

The rules are different. As nice as Ted was before things blew up, he ultimately did what many foxes do when the going got rough. He yelled. What should I have done? I should have been honest and let him have it.

Foxy **TIP**

Review all your smaller customers every six months and decide who should be getting preferential treatment.

Don't be a punching bag just because you're trying to deliver good service to the fox. Punch back. Foxes are grown-ups. And they're smart enough to realize when someone is being straight with them. Show your passion. Raise your voice. Be emphatic. You can do all this while still being professional and polite. But don't give some wooden response or canned speech when a fox is truly upset. He's in trouble. He's spent more than he planned. Something's not working. Help him figure out the problem and try not to mince words doing so. This is what a true partner would do.

Myth #4: "All customers are created equal."

Many companies that service large corporations have a few select customers that account for the lion's share of their revenues. In this case, one can set certain rules for treating each of these customers equally. In the crazy world of small business you're going to be dealing with many, many foxes on a thin margin so you can make a profit. These people are definitely not all created equal.

Ted should not have been treated the same as my other clients at the time. He needed more attention and I didn't give it to him. He deserved some extra hand holding and he didn't receive it. In our company, some clients get much better treatment than others. More often than not the customers that get treated better are the ones that are nice. It's certainly not easy serving hundreds of frenetic foxes. But it's much tougher to serve someone who's a difficult person.

All customers are certainly not created equal. The ones that pay on time, do what they say they're going to do, and are nice to work with, are the ones that are more equal than others. Ted could have been this kind of customer for us, but we didn't separate him from the pack. Thank goodness the small business market gives you lots of opportunities to find those great kinds of customers.

Myth #5: "You need to have a procedure for every situation."

A nice thought. But in the world of small business, too many policies are not necessarily a good thing at all. In fact, a plethora of customer service procedures may kill your profits. It's true that having good policies will create good customer service. But in the small business world it's important to have as few policies as possible. You shouldn't overregulate, and it's not possible to have a procedure for every situation.

Larger customers are used to their own internal policies and regulations. They sympathize with your policies. They understand the need for rules. They're more prepared to deal with your red tape just like they deal with their own red tape. This gives you the chance to really nail down a rigid system of customer service for the larger customer. Unfortunately, the small customer has the opposite approach.

A fox needs answers fast. He doesn't want to wade through a lot of red tape. He doesn't appreciate the rationale behind controls and procedures.

Your service organization should only have a few important rules. Give the discretion back to your service people to do the right thing and think on their feet. There are just too many unforeseen issues that can arise from servicing so many small business owners. You won't be able to come up with a response to each one. As long as you're not providing service to a rascal that owes you a lot of money or has been blacklisted for some other reason, you should respond quickly and accurately. Establish "customer policies and guidelines" but keep them extremely minimal. If we had less of these policies and more of an open response, I may have avoided Ted's ultimate tantrum.

Myth #6: "Always go the extra mile!"

Big customers with big revenue potential deserve the extra mile. Small customers with small dollar potential need to be evaluated carefully before putting yourself out.

We went the extra mile for Waterside. During the sales process we spent many hours with Ted's computer guy and even gave him a significant discount on the price of the software because we were promised that he had other clients that he could sell the software to. ("This is the beginning of what could be a very profitable long-term relationship," he had once told me happily.)

Foxy TIP

Always charge for your efforts, especially when you "go the extra mile." If a small customer complains about this, you can be the good guy by issuing a credit.

Once the project was underway we fielded all sorts of calls at all hours of the day and night from him. We traveled out of town to do on-site training with him. We had many hours of work that we didn't bill him for because he had made a good faith offer of future business. But then he suddenly disappeared from the scene. And then Ted asked us to do a lot more for nothing, or at the very least to take back the software we had sold him and provide him a full refund.

We had gone many extra miles for Ted and his company. Ted was only one of our many small business customers. I calculated the potential future long-term revenue stream from him if we were to comply with his requests. It wasn't much. I also calculated the potential future long-term investment I would have to make so that he would be happy. It was a lot. I saw a person who was not taking responsibility for a problem that he created. I decided not to go any more miles. I decided to stop entirely and give Ted his options: get help from us and pay us, find someone else, or do nothing. Ted ultimately decided to scrap his entire project. You will probably feel bad when a project doesn't work out. But you will feel worse if, by going the extra mile, you put yourself out of business for the sake of a fox who isn't responsible for himself.

Myth #7: "Underpromise and overdeliver."

"Underpromising" and "overdelivering" means nothing more than playing a game with your customer. And foxes don't like games. Many customer service gurus tell you to underpromise and overdeliver. Maybe this is true when dealing with larger customers. If a company is servicing technology at Citibank they might be able to get away with fuzzy commitments (i.e., underpromising everything that we will do) and then doing more than originally committed so that they look like heroes. This can be done when there's a larger contract to absorb any overages of time incurred to overdeliver what was originally committed to in the first place. There is also logic in this approach if you're competing against other firms for Citibank's business and you want to do something extra to stand out from the crowd. Or if the customer is a big enough plum for you and your company to really want to put out more effort than promised to keep them happy. If you're going to underpromise and over deliver then make sure it's to a "glass-is-half-empty" small customer. It may not be appreciated!

But underpromising and overdelivering isn't going to make you profitable in the small business environment. Ted's a good example. Should I have underpromised what the software would do or the services we would perform? Once the project was underway, should we have spent even more time and delivered more services than promised? Foxes, with limited budgets, need to know exactly what they're getting for their money. Most tend to be wary that someone is taking advantage of them. If we promised forty hours and delivered sixty hours, the wary fox tends to think that he overpaid us in the first place.

In the world of small business you really shouldn't play games. You'll be dealing with thin margins and have lots of fires to put out. There's little cushion like you might have with a larger customer's contract. You're most likely not going to be competing for work with three other vendors because the overworked fox doesn't have the time to maintain relationships with three other vendors. You're going to lose the customer if you don't do the job right or if your prices get too high. You will keep them happy if you do what you say you're going to do and get it done quickly. Don't underpromise the fox; just give them the facts. Don't overdeliver either, unless you like losing money.

Myth #8: "Always say yes!"

Most foxes are rarely happy about spending money. After all, who's truly happy about buying copy paper? Who jumps for joy when they pay their monthly phone bill? Satisfying the fox with your product or service is truly accomplishing something. Set your goals around satisfaction, not happiness, and you won't be disappointed with the results.

If you're only serving a small contingent of larger customers, you have the chance to focus your resources and efforts toward satisfying and making them happy. But in the world of small business you can't, and you won't, make *every* fox happy . . . or even satisfied. You're dealing with too many personalities. You're not going to be able to give as much attention to each fox as you would like, or that you would be able to do with a larger customer. You're going to have your share of "glass is half empty" foxes who always see the downside of things. You're going to run into those foxes, like Ted, who create their own problems despite your best efforts, and still blame you for their situation. A realistic goal is to shoot for an 80 percent satisfaction rate. That means that at any given time, one out of every five of your small business customers will not be satisfied with your products or service. Though this may fly in the face of traditional customer service wisdom, it's a great success ratio for this market.

Myth #9: "No news is good news."

For six weeks I hadn't heard a peep out of Ted. Hey, I thought to myself, everything must be just great; otherwise, I'd be hearing from him. No news is good news, right? Well, we all know the facts by now. While I was operating in ignorant bliss, this fox was becoming more and more agitated with each passing day. It wasn't until Ted called one of our service people and asked for help, and was refused (he had no time remaining on his service contract) that things finally boiled over. Managers in bigger companies may have, as policy, a process for giving feedback to their vendors. They like to fill out customer survey responses and consider it a productive part of their overall vendor relationship.

Busy foxes don't have a lot of time to keep their vendors informed. They're not into filling out questionnaires or giving feedback. They just want the things they bought to work. And because many of our heroes are willing to live with less than perfect products for less than retail prices, they won't tell you if there's a problem until it gets to be a big enough problem.

Don't assume that no news is good news. Keep close to the situation. You might be able to solve a potential problem before it became a much bigger problem. Never lay back and think that everything's okay just because no one's calling and complaining. Be more proactive with your foxes by calling and e-mailing them for updates. That way you can stay on top of their problems as they occur, not when they've festered into a much bigger sore.

Myth #10: "Get feedback from your customers!"

Nowadays, someone from a large corporation might think it unusual if they didn't receive some sort of customer feedback request after delivery. To big business, this is becoming a common step in the customer-vendor relationship. There's a huge industry of companies who facilitate customer feedback responses. Questionnaires, forms, Web pages, surveys . . . all of these things are meant to get feedback from customers to determine how satisfied they were with the service or product they received. It's all with the best of intentions and it certainly keeps a lot of people busy. I haven't analyzed this industry, but I imagine there's lots of great statistics about how important this all is and why everyone should be doing some type of customer satisfaction surveying.

Most foxes don't care about this. I've never sent a survey or a questionnaire to any of my foxes. We send invoices. And they pay them. By paying our invoices they tell me they're satisfied. With the fox, no matter what the contract says, you're going to have a tough time getting paid if your product or service isn't up to snuff. That's how he demonstrates satisfaction or unhappiness—he holds back the money. Make a point to review your open accounts receivable ledger frequently. If you see an amount pop into the over thirty-day column your antenna should immediately go up. The delay could be due to anything, but then again it could also be due to a genuine dissatisfaction with your products or service. Don't spend a lot of time or money with customer surveys. The fox's feedback form is his signature on a check.

Customer Service Tips That Will Make Your Foxes Love You

Now that we've dispensed with some of the more common customer service myths, we can turn to some proven practices that will help keep your small business customers coming back for more service. For example, Elasticon has been a client of ours for going on ten years. Elasticon, a 100-person manufacturer and distributor of plastic products, is owned and operated by two brothers, Kenneth and Darrell. They use our software products for their day-to-day operations and we provide periodic on-site service to support these applications and help out with some accounting tasks.

Elasticon is a pretty nutty place to work. The company has experienced significant growth and the two brothers push their employees to do as much as humanly possible in a day. Chaos reigns. Shouting matches often erupt. Kenneth and Darrell squabble, backstab, and bicker . . . yet they have a strong underlying mutual devotion. They both want what's best for the business and each other. Although we deal primarily with Kenneth, who has assumed the role of president, there's no question that we equally report to and are evaluated by Darrell. It's not an easy relationship to maintain, but somehow we've managed to do a pretty good job over the past years. We consider Elasticon to be one of our better clients.

There's always a personal element with every fox when you provide service. Unlike a larger company, where human contact can be constrained by formality, a relationship with the intrepid fox has a lot to do with how much you like each other. There are many reasons why we've profitably done business with Elasticon. We've employed certain practices over the years that have worked well with them, as well as many of our other foxes too. These practices are not myths, like the ones described above. They're tested and they work.

Service Tip #1: Cut to the chase and solve the problem

What's great about doing business with the fox is that you can leave most of your etiquette at the door and be very direct. For example, we've never beaten around the bush with Elasticon. We don't use the "underpromise and overdeliver" myth. Neither Kenneth nor Darrell have the time to play mind games. And my company doesn't have the budget to fool around with that we might have with a larger client. There are no levels of management to finesse. The owners of the company aren't afraid to have their feelings hurt like a big company employee might. They're more concerned with getting to the bottom of a problem and getting it fixed.

When Elasticon's receivables with their customers started to get too high, our systems brought this to the brothers' attention immediately and we all had a very direct (and loud) conversation about which partner was responsible for the problem. We then took actions for reducing the balance. When one brother's marital problems affected his performance on the job we addressed this sensitive issue together and agreed on a plan. Our directness and ability to offer suggestions to solve a problem was appreciated. Don't be afraid to be honest and direct with the crazy fox. He needs a partner, not a wimp. A corporate employee may need coddling, but a fox needs the truth.

Service Tip #2: Respond fast

An employee at a larger corporation may be used to waiting for things. He leaves messages for vendors, customers, and his fellow employees all the time. He's just performing a job. Things are rarely life and death, as long as it doesn't affect what time he leaves for the day or his upcoming vacation. But the fox operates differently. When one of the brothers at Elasticon asks an employee to get something done it's usually because it should have been done two weeks ago and now there's a panic. Foxes usually don't plan ahead like many corporate employees do. When you decide to do business with a bunch of foxes they're going to expect the same kind of response that their employees give them.

Your small business customers do not want to hear about your other customers or your problems. They want an immediate response. They'll get impatient very quickly. Whenever someone from Elasticon calls with a problem it really means there's a fire drill going on. We return the call as quickly as possible. It's a combination of self-respect and self-preservation. Respond immediately to your impatient foxes. They'll demand this kind of attention no matter how much they're paying you.

Service Tip #3: Check in for no reason at all

At small companies, things move very quickly. Foxes don't have the time to keep you updated about things that happen, even when you should know about them. If a larger client of ours decides to change its computer infrastructure you can be sure that we'll be asked to participate in the planning process to make sure all bases are covered. Not so with a small business.

For example, a few months ago, Elasticon's server began to slow down. Darrell hunted the Web and found a "great deal" on a new computer, which he promptly bought and attempted to set up on his own. Of course, things didn't work and the company's entire network went down. Luckily, I had just happened to e-mail Kenneth that day to check in and see how things were going. He mentioned that his lunatic brother bought this new computer and was intending to work on it that afternoon. My "uh-oh" antenna was suddenly activated. Sure enough, when things went south we were able to get out and help them right away.

To maintain the best level of service for the chaotic fox, your organization has to be proactive. You can't wait for something to happen because when it does it'll probably be some kind of a disaster requiring your immediate attention. And if you're not prepared to respond immediately then suddenly you may find yourself to be the culprit. Stay in close touch with your foxes. Use e-mail, the phone, and your fax machine to make sure no problems are brewing.

Service Tip #4: Be consistent

When I was a manager at a large accounting and consultancy firm, I specialized in "small" business clients. Because most of our clients fell among the largest companies in the world the definition of "small" still meant employing more than 1,000 people. Can you guess what the biggest complaint our firm received from its smaller clients? It wasn't our fees or our tough questions about their accounting practices. It was turnover. Our turnover. Our newest and less experienced people were automatically assigned to those accounts with the least amount of risk. My small business clients hated seeing a new face show up at their door every year to perform their audit and understand their business. They begged for continuity on their account. Turnover in my company affected my small business clients much more significantly than my larger clients.

While at this firm, my small business clients thought it extremely important that our staff return each year. Instead, because of the firm's staffing policy, these clients and I spent a great deal of time educating the new staff members on how their business works, where records were stored, and who to go to with questions. Repeating this process each year is costly. Our larger clients had more people to provide our staff with information and help them get up to speed. They were able to spread this knowledge among a greater number of people and make it easier for our staff to be productive more quickly. A fox must do all of that himself and this will not make him happy. Every time a vendor loses an employee the fox is affected. This kind of turnover could be a significant cost to companies like Elasticon.

Foxy TIP

Cross-train your employees so they can cover for each other when a small customer calls for help.

Service Tip #5: Let them win the battle, but not the war

Large customers bring with them large contracts. If there is a contract dispute or a problem with the job you may be talking about some serious money. For these kinds of customers it may very well be worth the effort to fight the battle.

Because most foxes are generally dealing in less significant amounts of money, you may often find yourself arguing over little stuff. Don, a small customer of mine argued over a two-hour service charge. The cost? Less than $100! One may hear "it's not the money, it's the principle" from a wily fox like Don but take it from me: for most foxes, it's almost always about the money! If it's so important for that customer to get a $100 reduction in his bill, you may want to consider letting him have it, even if he is completely out of line. You can get it back in some way later on and he'll feel like he won one.

In a dispute like the one we had with Don, I took the high road and let him decide what was right. I committed myself to abiding by his decision, even though I disagreed. It settled the issue and let us move forward. Give the fox a sense of control. This is what they're used to having. And it shows respect for his decision, which is also what foxes want from their partners.

Service Tip #6: Do stuff for free

Foxes really appreciate getting something for nothing. Every dollar you save the fox directly impacts his livelihood. Employees at larger companies are less impacted by "freebies" and generally are less excited by these efforts.

When things at my company are slow I send out some of my technicians to clients to do service work at no charge. For example, Kenneth and Darrell had purchased a software utility from us that sends alerts whenever an accounts receivable invoice goes overdue. They never got around to setting up the program and it just laid there for many, many months. One week we had some open time on our schedule and I sent one of our technicians out to install the software and configure it so that e-mails were sent to the brothers as their customers' invoices became overdue. I didn't charge them for the technician's time. It cost me about $1,000. But I got two great benefits from it.

First, my technician spent the available time getting to know this application so he could use this knowledge, in a paying capacity, at another client at some other point of time. And second, the brothers at Elasticon were all thrilled to get this software working and really appreciated that we didn't charge them for the extra time to do it. They got something for free. This may not seem a lot for a larger company. But for a small business, saving $1,000 is a lot of money. And how often does a fox actually have someone do something for them without asking for anything back? Good will does go a long way.

Service Tip #6: Service your best foxes first, and weed out the rest

In a recent article on business, the author insisted that all customers should be treated like gold. Maybe that's true for big customers with large contracts. But with many foxes you're going to have to separate the gold from the silver and the silver from the lead. Life is not fair. Some customers are more equal than others. Reward your best foxes.

Elasticon is one of our very best small business clients and not because they are our largest. They pay us a fixed monthly amount, and, frankly, some months we don't make much, if any profit, on their account. But they are a longtime client. They pay their bills on time. They've given us special projects that have been worthwhile. They're loyal users of our software products. They treat our staff with respect.

In addition to Elasticon, we have a bunch of great foxes that we truly enjoy doing business with. These customers always seem to receive that little something extra from us. Unfortunately, we have other foxes that we don't especially like. These rogues often do not get the benefit of the doubt.

There are a lot of foxes out there to work with. Twice a year, look at your client list to see which clients don't fit into your mold and try to replace them. This is not easy and it would be stupid to drop a good paying, profitable customer just because you don't like them. But you should strive to keep the majority of your small business customers in line with your own culture.

Summary

Many of the things that experts may have told you are true when it comes to delivering high-quality customer service are not applicable to the crazy and cunning fox. Although this advice may be applicable when servicing larger organizations, much of it doesn't hold water in the small business environment.

Even with a great client you need to keep in mind that you're only as good as the last thing you've done. Foxes are good people, but they're also people trying to run a small company. They're beset by their own financial and other business woes every day. They may express some interest in your business but it's not their primary concern.

Small business owners are only concerned with what you have done for them lately. Your service may be great this month but can easily falter the next. You may think things are going swimmingly, but behind the scenes your customer is angry with you because of something you said. The resourceful fox, different from the company manager, has the ability to make changes and sever relationships quickly. He has no approval process or team members to consult. If he finds something better, or more importantly cheaper, you could easily be yesterday's news.

So when providing your services to the demanding fox don't let yourself get too extended. Get your money. Pay attention to any warning signs. Always keep the quality level as high as you can to keep your foxes satisfied—but not so high that it affects your slim margins, unless you charge for the added value.

Too Big for Their Britches

How to Part Ways with Your Small Customers

I got a call from Glen, the newly appointed chief financial officer of the startup, DataMart, Inc. He was looking for some accounting software for his company. Just another small business? Not DataMart!

He got my name from his tax accountant who was a mutual acquaintance. At the time, I thought the call was kind of strange. What kind of small company has a chief financial officer, for goodness sakes? Well, I definitely got an education. I've learned that when a startup company already has an appointed chief financial officer, I should be prepared for a small business that's really not a small business. DataMart fit the bill.

This was no typical mom-and-pop. Glen and his four partners all came from a large database marketing company with the idea of starting a niche company that would provide not only data to its customers, but telemarketing services, and consulting as well. Not a bad idea. In fact, the idea was good enough to attract more than a million dollars in seed funding and Glen was out talking to the venture capital community for more. I can think of quite a few little foxes that wouldn't mind that kind of dough to help them finance their companies. I thought that these big company guys would go down in flames. What did they know about running a small business? Quite a bit, apparently. DataMart was not going to be small for long. From the very first days of its operation, DataMart was destined to become a big business.

And it did. Over the next two years, the company's revenues grew from nothing to more than $10 million per year. By the time DataMart and I amicably parted ways, Glen had hired a full-time corporate controller and two accounting staff members to round out his finance department. The company had moved offices twice, finally relocating to a high-rent professional office tower outside of New York. The original accounting system they had purchased from me was replaced by a more robust application to handle complex time and billing and deferred revenue transactions.

DataMart has continued to grow and is in the final stages of an initial public offering. Soon there will be millions in its coffers to fund its expansion. Glen and his partners have done a great job. Their original investors will walk from this adventure happy and wealthy.

I know this because I've been keeping in touch with Glen. I'm happy to admit that I called this one correctly from the beginning. It was obvious that DataMart, although small when we first started doing business together, did not fit the typical definition of the small business we usually served. I sold them entry-level accounting software and provided them with certain services that Glen needed at the time. But both Glen and I were clear with each other that our relationship was going to end when DataMart became too big. I planned for the inevitable. I helped them with the transition to their new system. And I continue to keep in touch with Glen to this day. We began and ended our business relationship on good terms.

The Three Paths a Fox Can Take

There will be a lot of foxes who come and go in your life. It's only natural. In the small business market, where volume is the name of the game, you're going to be doing business with many customers. Some will stay customers for a long time. Others won't.

A new customer may not stay a customer forever. Statistically, my company turns over about one in ten customers a year. This means that at the end of each year, we've lost about 10 percent of our small customers that were with us at the beginning of the year. I've come to expect this. When everyone is kissing and hugging each other at the beginning of the relationship I'm already thinking about the ways things can head south. Typically, a relationship with a small business customer will take one of the following paths.

The Satisfied Forever Path

In this scenario, the customer stays a customer forever. It is commonplace for a company to turn over about 10 percent of their customer base a year. Even the smartest, wackiest and wiliest foxes find it satisfactory to stay with us for years. As long as the fox gets satisfactory products and services, he'll keep coming back for more. This does not mean that there won't be bumps in the road. Expect them. In fact, you should purposely not use the word "happy," because there probably aren't that many people who are really jumping for joy over your product (unless you're a chocolate maker!). Be happy with "satisfied." The long-term customer is what we all strive for, isn't it? You want most of your small customers to stick with you on a "satisfied" forever path.

The Divorce

Unfortunately, some of your relationships will not end happily ever after. And when they do end, it can sometimes get a little ugly. The crazy fox may blame you for every woe they've ever experienced, every shift in the marketplace, and every downturn in their business. Or it could be that the resourceful fox has figured out a cheaper way to do things and doesn't need you any more. Then there are those foxes that simply don't like you, your company, your products, or your services. These foxes will part ways from you, sometimes bitterly, and may claim poor quality, bad service, nonresponsiveness, and high prices. They might be right, but usually it's something that's not in your control. In the small business market you have to grow a thick skin and accept the fact that some customers will not stay customers.

Growing Pains

Sometimes your small business customers will simply outgrow you and move on to bigger and better things. Like DataMart, the services you provide may no longer be necessary. The company may become too big for you to handle. As we've discussed earlier, many of these kinds of customers can be spotted in advance, so at least you have a chance to prepare for the inevitable separation.

These are the only three paths that a customer relationship can take. Some customers will stay with you forever, and some will leave you in disgust. There will also be some foxes that do like you, but will leave you anyway. That's because they become big bears. Their wishes outstrip your offerings. Your business isn't organized to serve them appropriately. Your products fall short of their needs.

Wouldn't it be nice to identify those kinds of small businesses as early as possible? That way you can serve them for as long as possible, but still prepare yourself for an amicable separation that may lead to future referrals and good will.

Will That Little Fox Be a Big Bear One Day?

Some small businesses, such as DataMart, are destined to be large right from the beginning. Others just evolve and grow over time. At some point, you may find yourself selling products or services to a very different organization than you once knew. You may wake up one day and discover that one of your small business customers has suddenly turned into a corporate customer, and that you're not organized to meet their needs. That would be a shame. It's a much better scenario when you identify those small customers early on and prepare for the future. Is there any way to tell when a little fox may one day turn into a big bear? There are certain warning signs that are certain indications of danger ahead.

Warning Sign #1: Invasion of the Big Company Managers!

A lot of times small companies are started by refugees from bigger companies. In the case of DataMart, it wasn't just one manager but four executives who all came from the same corporate background. None of them had experience running a company themselves. Though smart in big company ways, they were not resourceful like the typical fox. Many times big company managers either start a small business to grow it into another big company or intend to keep it super small, almost like a hobby.

At DataMart, these former big company managers brought with them the culture and attitude of their former employer.

They viewed certain things as necessity: a good location, administrative staff, top-flight office furniture, etc. Most thrifty foxes would scratch their heads at this model. But if these ex-big company guys were going to do this venture, they were going to do it right and not cut any corners. Keep your eyes on those former corporate managers–turned–foxes. Their presence may be a sign of a small company poised to become big.

Warning Sign #2: Big Bucks Behind the Scenes

DataMart was no shoestring operation. Unlike the typical small business, money wasn't hoarded from vendors, on loan from relatives, or borrowed from some local bank. While still working at their former jobs, our heroes at DataMart created a formal business plan. They knew how to play the game and succeeded by receiving seed funding from a venture capital organization. Many foxes could use financing to grow their business. But most of these foxes don't have the time, the education, or the *savoir-faire* to market themselves to outside investors. In addition many small business owners are suspicious of outside interference and don't want to involve other parties in their affairs. Thus, they never get the money to really grow and inevitably stay small.

After years of working at a big company, the managers from DataMart had no reservations about working with third parties if it meant getting the money they needed to turn DataMart into a substantial business. It's important to realize that when venture capital firms or professional investors have a stake in a small company, the company is destined not to stay small. Venture capitalists don't invest in pizza shops. They want a 30 percent return and quickly. DataMart was a small company about to become big.

Warning Sign #3: The Cream Rises to the Top

DataMart was definitely a top-heavy little company. This was a sure sign of a small company trying to become big. We've discussed lots of smart foxes who run their businesses themselves, with little help from others. Many of these foxes solely bear the burden of finance, marketing, sales, and operations. But DataMart had a different approach, right from the beginning. The four executives who started the company were all equal partners and were used to managing staffs beneath them. None of them had the management skills, or the fox-like attributes, to run their own company. They pooled their resources for the purposes of putting together a good-looking management team that could be packaged and sold to outside investors. They planned to hire employees who would do the actual work once the money was raised.

It was a strategy that worked. Investors liked DataMart's business plan and took an equity position based on the future objectives. Few small businesses are organized this way. DataMart stood out right from the beginning. I learned that a small company with too many managers may either lack a smart fox at the helm or may be on the cusp of becoming a larger company.

Warning Sign #4: Overstaffed and Underworked

As crazy as some of the foxes I work with are, they would look at me like I was a lunatic if I suggested hiring a marketing manager. Or, heaven forbid, the thought of hiring a human resources person. Why go to the expense? Where's the return? What's the point?

The fearless crew at DataMart didn't feel the same way. Being big company people they brought big company ways with them to DataMart. They hired positions that don't exist at many medium-sized companies—let alone small businesses. A Marketing Manager? Most of little foxes I work with consider an ad in their monthly church bulletin to be a cutting-edge marketing practice. A Human Resources director? What for? You got your paycheck, didn't you? Glen and his partners at DataMart had a different outlook. If they were going to grow, they needed to put the right people in place now, not later.

Luckily, Glen and his partners had the financing to prepare themselves for their inevitable growth and put these people in place. Small companies that have people in corporate-type positions are positioning themselves to become larger companies. If a little company has a big corporate structure then it's a small business that is not looking to stay that way.

Warning Sign #5: Wow! Who's Your Decorator?

Most crazy foxes would rather sink their money into an addition on their own house than fix up their office space. Sure, having nice office space would be great, but who's going to pay those high rents? The resourceful fox keeps his facility clean and presentable, but doesn't go overboard. It's just an office, for goodness sakes.

Not so for the small company destined to be big. Glen and his team were used to working in offices with plush carpeting and designer furniture. They certainly weren't going to step down the ladder of success now. DataMart's partners had a vision for their company, and that vision did not include operating out of an industrial park. They saw themselves in an office with nice carpets, a reception area, elevators, a doorman, and classical music piped through an invisible sound system. And that's what they leased. After all they weren't paying for it, their investors were. If you walk into a small company with really nice offices it should be a red flag that there is no wily little fox running the show. Something else is going on. It's is a small business that wants to be a big business. Maybe it'll succeed, like DataMart. Or maybe this façade will turn out to be waste of money. But in any case the fox at the helm wants to be a big bear someday.

Warning Sign #6: Outside Accountants and Lawyers That Bill More Than $200 an Hour

See that short little guy with the mustache, thinning hair, rumpled sweater and old sneakers walking toward his car carrying a cardboard box full of receipts? That's what a typical small business accountant looks like. He's going back to his office to place the box alongside of dozens of other boxes belonging to other mom-and-pops he services. Hey, don't knock him. For $50 an hour he'll give you a tax return, a quick financial statement, and ten reasons why the current administration isn't worth a damn.

DataMart, and other small companies looking to be large, don't usually employ this kind of accountant. They're gearing up for the majors, so that means they must hire major league accountants and lawyers. These are the types of professionals whose interns charge you $200 an hour. Small companies that want to grow big associate themselves with the big professional firms—the types of firms that have connections in the investment community and cachet on Wall Street. Most resourceful foxes care more about saving a few bucks than positioning themselves with the investment community. But for those few small companies destined for greatness, this is the game they must play. Whenever you bump into a Big Four accounting firm or high-priced lawyers at a prospective small customer, you may be working with a company that will quickly outgrow your product or services.

Warning Sign #7: A Stock Compensation Plan for Employees

Most small businesses are privately owned, proprietorships, or S-Corporations with a few shares signed over to their name. DataMart, I quickly found out, was organized differently. Glen and his team had elaborately structured the company with "common" and "preferred" stock. They issued thousands of shares and set up compensation plans to issue more shares if certain goals were met. They spent a great deal of time with their big-time lawyers and accountants setting up this equity structure. They even came up with a stock compensation plan for their current and future employees! DataMart was not your typical small business.

The typical fox is trying his best to survive and succeed. He's loath to give up equity in his company. He works too hard to give it all away to someone else. He's not going to spend the time creating complex stockholder equity and compensation plans, especially when he's the sole stockholder.

Warning Sign #8: Doing Business Nationally and Internationally

There are many courageous, and sometimes very wily, little foxes working the tricky world of international customs, duties, freight and taxes in order to do business outside of their home country. That type of trade can be very profitable, as long as one pays attention to all those extra little costs and keeps his shipping insurance premiums up to date. Most crazy foxes prefer to work in their own backyard.

Not so with big companies. Big companies are used to dealing with foreign offices and international customers. At the very least they are probably doing business in most of North America. If your small customer is working to build an international presence, by creating foreign offices and hiring people in different parts of the world, this is a sign the company intends to grow. This may be a company destined to grow on an international scale. Look for this sign when evaluating your prospective small business customers.

Warning Sign #9: Executive Perks Are High

Oh, those big company execs—they sure love to party, don't they? Corporate apartments, generous bonus plans, hired jets, first class travel, restricted stock grants, fancy lunches, company cars . . . you know the rest.

Everyone complains about these over-the-top excesses, but we're all envious, aren't we? Small business owners are no different. Any of my customers would tell you that he'd rather be driven to work in a limo then fight traffic in his '98 Explorer. Bonus plan? This crazy fox just got payment from his customer and it was only five days late. Now *that's* what a typical fox would call a bonus!

Glen and his friends took great care to set up the right compensation plans at the very early stages of his company. Clearly, DataMart had big aspirations in mind. They were not going to be the usual mom-and-pop store. Funding these types of perks means that there had better be some pretty significant revenue forecasts. Revenue that can only be found at a larger company, not a small one.

Warning Sign #10: Financial Reporting Is Like a Public Company

I remember receiving our reporting instructions from Glen when we started working with him. Pages of monthly reports and analysis were required for the executive team and their investors. Profit and Loss, Cash Flows, Depreciation, Backlog, Collections . . . all of this information was needed right away to put into a financial reporting package for investors. Clearly, Glen was positioning his financial reports not only for his immediate investors, but also for the future investors that would be looking at his company. On the advice of his big-time accountants, he had us create financial statements that mirrored the same kind of reports that would be required in public offering documents and future filings with the Securities and Exchange Commission.

Most of the crazy foxes I know look at one report every month . . . their bank statement! Then at the end of the year they look at their tax return, complain that they didn't make any money, yet they're paying a bunch of taxes, and leave their reporting at that.

It was clear from his financial reporting structure that Glen was positioning his little company to be much bigger. If a prospective little customer has big-company reporting requirements you're probably dealing with a big company in the making.

Passing the Baton—How to Terminate Your Relationship Successfully

Whenever you start a relationship with a new fox, whether resourceful, wacky, or a rascal, you should think ahead to how the relationship may end. Some of your small customers, like DataMart, are destined to be big companies. Other rascals may force you to prematurely terminate your relationship through no fault of your own. And of course there will be those crazy foxes that accuse you of every crime on earth and vow never to do business with you again.

In the small business market, you'll be dealing with a lot of little customers and you're not going to keep them all. Extricating yourself from an unwanted relationship can be costly, distracting, and time-consuming. Like DataMart, some customers give you red flags way in advance that you'll one day be parting ways. Other little foxes may not be so easy to figure out. But the better you are at predicting the outcome of your relationships, the more profitably you'll be able to exit the stage and move on to a more favorable customer. Here are some suggestions for professionally ending your relationship with these types of small business owners while at the same time keeping your head high and minimizing your costs.

Have a Spectacular Exit Plan

For DataMart, it was pretty obvious from the beginning that we wouldn't be serving them for the long term. Besides companies like DataMart, I've done business with a fair share of foxes that I knew from the beginning would most likely not work out. In fact, I recently started a project with a wacky little fox named Jennifer who hired us to install an accounting system in her three-person office. I know for a fact that she had a big dispute with her former accounting system vendor. She danced around our agreements and my phone calls, even before the project began. And yet I'm still going to give it a shot with her, because sometimes I'm just as crazy as she is! I know full well that the job could end in tears. But here's the important thing: I've already thought up an exit plan in case things really do head south. I'm prepared for the worst and ready to minimize my losses.

Coming up with a spectacular exit plan well in advance will save you time when and if the relationship hits the fan. For my crazy customer, Jennifer, I structured our agreement to deliver specific things in checklist format and the minute we've delivered I plan to stop all work. Jennifer can be a little rascal and I fully expect her to try and squeeze out more work for no money. However, I know in advance that I'm not going to be very flexible with her. I know in advance that I'm going to be pretty tough and not negotiate very much. Different clients require different approaches. The minute I see smoke, I plan to make sure all our commitments were delivered per the checklist and then pull back the troops until Jennifer and I agree on additional funding. I've decided these issues now so I won't be taken off guard later. We may lose her as a client because of this plan, but I'm prepared for the consequences.

Don't Burn Bridges!

Your small business customers will be resourceful, smart, crazy, and sometimes tricky, but never forget one thing: they'll always be around. Small business owners are survivors. Few ever go back into the corporate world once they've been out on their own.

So when you terminate a relationship with your small business customer, do your best to do it professionally. Don't burn bridges. It's a small world out there. The theory about "six degrees of separation" between people is accurate. We're all separated from each other by a very few connections. That scoundrel you parted ways with may bump into you a few months later at a baseball game. The lunatic that you vowed never to do business with again may suddenly join forces with one of your customers. The smart foxes will continue to be out there and you're going to see them again. Make sure your exit plan takes the high road and that you don't burn any bridges.

Introduce a Replacement

If you're going to part ways with a customer, be it amicable or not, offer someone in your place. Even if your small business customer turns out to be the rascal that you feared he would be, don't leave them in the lurch. Graciously offer them some names of your competitors that they could do business with. DataMart outgrew my firm quickly, but not before I had the chance to introduce them to some of the larger applications and vendors that would be appropriate for them down the road. It's the right thing to do to help out a former client.

Drop a Big Hint by Raising Your Prices

The best way to end your relationship with any fox is to raise your prices so much that the fox can't afford you any more. It's an effective exit plan. If things go badly with Jennifer, as may very well happen, my exit plan includes a pricing change. She doesn't know this yet. If I feel that we've completed everything as agreed on the checklist, and she still behaves unreasonably and tries to squeeze more free services out of me, then I'll be ready. I built a wide range of hourly rates in our service contract with her (which she ultimately did sign). I'm ready to offer her additional services if she desires, but at a much higher rate.

Always Give Options

The choice to exit shouldn't be yours. It should be your customers'. Let them decide. Give them options. And for the really tough ones, nudge them in the right direction.

If your small business customer begins to outgrow you, or if your relationship is turning sour, give him some choices. This is not *The Godfather*. You're not going to make him an offer he can't refuse. In times of transition, all emotions must be put aside and you should try and think of what's best for the customer, even if that means becoming a former customer. Make sure your options are documented and communicated clearly. No one, especially an attorney, should be in a position to come back and accuse you of not acting in the best interests of their client. Small business owners like their independence. They want to exercise their freedom of choice. Give them the chance to display their free will.

The Relationship Never Ends

It's extremely important to end a relationship with a small business customer amicably. Granted, this isn't possible all the time. But you should make every attempt to end things on the most positive note possible. We ended our relationship with DataMart, but still use them for future referrals. In fact, they're a great referral for prospective small customers that I think may one day become big, just like DataMart. Because we've kept on good terms with Glen it's become a real asset to show a potential client that we will work with them from the very beginning and help them transition when the situation requires. Having big companies as a reference brings creditability and intangible value.

If you're able to keep an amicable relationship in place with a former customer then you can maintain relationships with their employees. Thus if an employee leaves that customer and takes a job somewhere else, he or she may be able to give you new business through their new employer.

Summary

Have you noticed something special about DataMart? Something different from the typical fox we've talked about in this book? Glen and his partners came from a big company, raised venture financing, started up a little company and grew it into something big. They also did this over a relatively short period of time. They were top-heavy, hired management early, rented nice office space, and created a big company long before it was a big company. I never considered DataMart to be a small business. I really never considered Glen and his partners to be small businessmen either.

For starters, they didn't have the independent and survivalist nature that most of my small business customers have. They didn't leave their jobs until they had millions in venture funding. They knew that after receiving the first round of financing, their chances of future rounds were very much assured. In some ways, it was if they were taking on new jobs rather than starting up a new company. Their new employers were their investors. These guys weren't survivors. They were employees.

They weren't very crazy either. I never heard shouting or yelling in their offices. No plates were thrown. No tears were shed. Definitely not like my typical small customers. They kept business-like hours and always behaved in a professional manner, never letting their hair down. They dressed in corporate attire. They were just like all the big company employees I've encountered. They sat at their desks and conducted their jobs just like they did at the company where they previously worked.

And finally, these guys really weren't rascals either. They didn't cut corners or take shortcuts. I never saw them taking advantage of a vendor playing a sneaky payment delay trick. They knew they had investors looking over their shoulders every day.

The partners at DataMart weren't little foxes at all. They didn't share the most common traits of small business owners. They weren't resourceful, crazy or sneaky enough to stay a small business owner forever.

Terminating your relationship with some of your small business customers will be common practice when you're dealing with so many of them. On any given day you're going to have confrontations with a little fox. Sometimes you'll be at fault. Other times it'll just be because the fox is a wily creature. But don't worry; there are a lot of others out there, crazy as they are. And there's a lot of money to be made from all those crazy foxes.

Index

publicity, threat of bad, 160–61
purchasing power, 16–18

R

references, 220
referrals, 64–65
resources, lack of, 12–13
respect, 74
response time, 197–98
return on investment (ROI), 80–81
revenues, 6

S

sales
  breaking down, for payment,
    147–48
  follow-up, 156–59
sales objections. *See* objections
satisfaction rates, 193–94
schedules, 14, 176
self-confidence, lack of, 169–71
selling
  cookie-cutter approach to, 79
  vs. educating, 59–60
service desks
  hours of, 176
  need for, 174, 175–76
  software for, 177–78
service issues, 163–82
  laws for success, 172–74
  tools needed for, 174–81
  unique challenges, 165–71
skepticism, 86
small businesses
  companies selling to, 4–5
  defining, 6–12
  enormity of, 49–50
  information about, 8–9
  low profile of, 11–12
  marketing to, 45–67
  ownership of, 8

statistics on, 4, 17, 21, 49, 57, 63,
    71, 81, 94, 101
  terminating relationship with,
    216–20
  that turn into big businesses,
    209–16
  top problems for, 25
small business owners
  See also customers
  characteristics of, vii–xi , 20–21
  communication styles of, 167–68
  connecting with, 71–72
  vs. corporate customers, 4–5,
    12–18
  as decision makers, 48–49, 57–58,
    100–101
  demands made by, 18–19
  disqualifying, 69–87
  evaluating, 40–43
  flexibility of, 171
  friendships with, 149
  know-it-all, 29–31
  lack of professionalism in,
    36–38
  long-term relationships with,
    19–20, 158–59
  with negative attitudes, 38–40,
    193–94
  parting ways with, 205–22
  personal responsibility of, 14
  reaching, 18–20
  relationships with, 207–9
  service issues with, 163–82
  seven types of, 23–42
  statistics on, 83, 96, 164, 188
  successful, 24–26
  sympathy for, 143
  types to avoid, 83–86
software
  communications, 178
  contact management, 145–46
  help desk, 177–78